D1552035

1st EDITION

Perspectives on Modern World History

The Munich Olympics Massacre

1st EDITION

Perspectives on Modern World History

The Munich Olympics Massacre

Jeff Hay

Editor

GREENHAVEN PRESS
A part of Gale, Cengage Learning

Detroit • New York • San Francisco • New Haven, Conn • Waterville, Maine • London

GALE
CENGAGE Learning·

Elizabeth Des Chenes, *Director, Content Strategy*
Cynthia Sanner, *Publisher*
Douglas Dentino, *Manager, New Product*

For more information, contact:
Greenhaven Press
27500 Drake Rd.
Farmington Hills, MI 48331-3535
Or you can visit our Internet site at gale.cengage.com.

For product information and technology assistance, contact us at
Gale Customer Support, 1-800-877-4253.

For permission to use material from this text or product, submit all requests online at
www.cengage.com/permissions.

Further permissions questions can be e-mailed to permissionrequest@cengage.com.

Articles in Greenhaven Press anthologies are often edited for length to meet page requirements. In addition, original titles of these works are changed to clearly present the main thesis and to explicitly indicate the author's opinion. Every effort is made to ensure that Greenhaven Press accurately reflects the original intent of the authors. Every effort has been made to trace the owners of copyrighted material.

Cover image © Hulton Archive/Getty Images and © ArtisticPhoto/Shutterstock.com.

LIBRARY OF CONGRESS CATALOGING-IN-PUBLICATION DATA

The Munich Olympics massacre / Jeff Hay, book editor.
    pages cm. -- (Perspectives on modern world history)
    Includes bibliographical references and index.
    ISBN 978-0-7377-6369-0 (hardcover)
1. Olympic Games (20th : 1972 : Munich, Germany) 2. Athletes--Violence a gainst--Germany--Munich. 3. Israelis--Violence against--Germany--Munich. 4 . Terrorism--Germany--Munich. I. Hay, Jeff.
    HV6433.G3M86 2014
    364.152'30943364--dc23   2013035190

CONTENTS

Twenty-five years afterward, a writer speaks with renowned ABC sports announcer Jim McKay, who remained in front of the cameras for hours on September 5, 1972.

CHAPTER 2: Controversies Surrounding the Munich Olympics Massacre

closely connected to the Munich attack asserts that the Palestinians gained a victory by bringing their plight to the attention of millions around the world.

CHAPTER 3: Personal Narratives

Olympics, a sports journalist writes of his personal reactions to the 1972 terrorist attacks.

FOREWORD

"History cannot give us a program for the future, but it can give us a fuller understanding of our-selves, and of our common humanity, so that we can better face the future."
—Robert Penn Warren,
American poet and novelist

The history of each nation is punctuated by momentous events that represent turning points for that nation, with an impact felt far beyond its borders. These events—displaying the full range of human capabilities, from violence, greed, and ignorance to heroism, courage, and strength—are nearly always complicated and multifaceted. Any student of history faces the challenge of grasping the many strands that constitute such world-changing events as wars, social movements, and environmental disasters. But understanding these significant historic events can be enhanced by exposure to a variety of perspectives, whether of people involved intimately or of ones observing from a distance of miles or years. Understanding can also be increased by learning about the controversies surrounding such events and exploring hot-button issues from multiple angles. Finally, true understanding of important historic events involves knowledge of the events' human impact—of the ways such events affected people in their everyday lives—all over the world.

Perspectives on Modern World History examines global historic events from the twentieth century onward by presenting analysis and observation from numerous vantage points. Each volume offers high school, early college level, and general interest readers a thematically arranged anthology of previously published materials that address a major historical event, with an emphasis on international coverage. Each volume opens with background information on the event, then presents the controversies surrounding that event, and concludes with first-person narratives from people who lived through the event or were affected by it. By providing primary sources from the time of the event, as well as relevant commentary surrounding the event, this series can be used to inform debate, help develop critical thinking skills, increase global awareness, and enhance an understanding of international perspectives on history.

Material in each volume is selected from a diverse range of sources, including journals, magazines, newspapers, nonfiction books, personal narratives, speeches, congressional testimony, government documents, pamphlets, organization newsletters, and position papers. Articles taken from these sources are carefully edited and introduced to provide context and background. Each volume of Perspectives on Modern World History includes an array of views on events of global significance. Much of the material comes from international sources and from US sources that provide extensive international coverage.

Each volume in the Perspectives on Modern World History series also includes:

- A full-color **world map**, offering context and geographic perspective.
- An annotated **table of contents** that provides a brief summary of each essay in the volume.
- An **introduction** specific to the volume topic.
- For each viewpoint, a brief **introduction** that has notes about the author and source of the viewpoint, and that provides a summary of its main points.
- Full-color **charts**, **graphs**, **maps**, and other visual representations.

- Informational **sidebars** that explore the lives of key individuals, give background on historical events, or explain scientific or technical concepts.
- A **glossary** that defines key terms, as needed.
- A **chronology** of important dates preceding, during, and immediately following the event.
- A **bibliography** of additional books, periodicals, and websites for further research.
- A comprehensive **subject index** that offers access to people, places, and events cited in the text.

Perspectives on Modern World History is designed for a broad spectrum of readers who want to learn more about not only history but also current events, political science, government, international relations, and sociology—students doing research for class assignments or debates, teachers and faculty seeking to supplement course materials, and others wanting to improve their understanding of history. Each volume of Perspectives on Modern World History is designed to illuminate a complicated event, to spark debate, and to show the human perspective behind the world's most significant happenings of recent decades.

INTRODUCTION

I n 1969 an American-born attorney named David Berger moved to Israel, hoping to start a law practice there. He also hoped to compete for the Israeli Olympic team. Berger was born to a wealthy family living in a suburb of Cleveland, Ohio. He was a standout student and athlete at both the high school and college levels. A weightlifter, Berger competed throughout his years of schooling at amateur competitions. After moving to Israel, marrying, and finishing his required military service, Berger won a silver medal for Israel at the 1971 Asian Weightlifting Championships. He was a logical choice for Israel's Olympic team.

In August 1972 Berger and his teammates traveled to Munich, West Germany, to take part in the twentieth Olympic Games. He and ten of his comrades never returned. They died as the result of a botched kidnapping attempt carried out by Palestinian terrorists. The Munich Olympics massacre—which resulted in the deaths of eleven Israelis, one West German policeman, and five terrorists—remains the greatest tragedy of the modern Olympic Games. It also was a defining event in the contemporary history of terrorism.

The terrorists who attacked David Berger and his teammates at Munich belonged to a group that called itself Black September. Formed just a year earlier, Black September consisted mostly of activists who already belonged to one of several offshoots of the larger Palestine Liberation Organization (PLO), notably the radical Fatah wing. Only in recent years had Palestinians turned to launching terrorist attacks outside their region, and Black September continued that effort. The group took shape when the Kingdom of Jordan expelled PLO leaders and many ordinary refugees beginning in September 1971. Palestinians were dismayed, since Jordan had previously been the friendliest of all the Arab states to Palestinian refugees. The militants who joined Black September not only hoped for vengeance against Jordanians, who indeed became their first victims, but also to draw attention to what they saw as the hopelessness of Palestinian refugees. In the early 1970s few around the world seemed to care about the hundreds of thousands of Palestinians who were displaced in the years since the nation of Israel was founded in 1948.

In the summer of 1972 a Black September leader who called himself Abu Daoud suggested that an attack on the upcoming Olympic Games in Munich might help bring the fate of Palestinians to the world's notice. Since the Olympics were a worldwide event, the games would be broadcast around the globe using new satellite TV technology, and an attack there would obviously have a great impact. Daoud's plan called for the group to kidnap members of Israel's Olympic delegation and then exchange them for Palestinians held in Israeli jails. In later interviews Daoud asserted that the plan never called for the killing of any hostages.

Meanwhile, in Munich, what West Germans hoped would be the "Happy Games" began with the Olympic opening ceremony on August 26, 1972. The Germans wanted to make a special effort to draw a contrast between these Olympics and the last ones held in Germany, the so-called "Nazi Olympics" of 1936 in Berlin. Security guards and Munich police assigned to the event were not in uniform and instead wore simple light-blue shirts. They also were unarmed. The Olympic Village, where athletes stayed, was not strongly guarded: It was surrounded only by a single chain-link fence that could easily be climbed over, and little attention was paid to who went in and out of the gates in the fence. The lack of security precautions has been blamed as one cause of the

Munich massacre, but 1972 was in a different era than the early twenty-first century; athletes at Munich noted that security was not much different at the 1964 games in Tokyo and the 1968 competition in Mexico City.

Early in the morning of September 5, 1972, eight Black September terrorists entered the Olympic Village. They were wearing athletic warm-ups and carrying weapons in sports bags, and they apparently were helped over the fence by friendly Americans who had been out on the town. Shortly afterward, the terrorists entered an apartment building where part of the Israeli delegation was housed. In their initial assault two Israelis were killed, and while a number of others were able to escape, nine athletes and coaches were taken hostage.

Negotiations over the fate of the hostages took place over several hours on September 5. Israel's government refused to make deals with terrorists, and with no other government stepping forward, it fell to the West Germans and Olympic officials to try to resolve the crisis. Meanwhile outside the building where the hostages were held, the events largely continued as normal. Athletes relaxed, or trained, and visitors continued to enjoy the scene. The rest of the world, however, was paying close attention as TV sportscasters found themselves transformed into political reporters and as a live television feed reached millions.

A German plan to use sharpshooters in the Olympic Village was eventually abandoned. Instead, negotiators agreed to take the hostages and the terrorists to a military airport at Fürstenfeldbruck on the outskirts of Munich. From there all would be flown to an Arab country where, hopefully, negotiations for an exchange of hostages could continue. The West Germans, however, continued with plans for some kind of armed resolution to the crisis. Snipers were placed all around the airport, and an armed crew was stationed on the aircraft that was to take the hostages and terrorists out of Germany.

The West German plan collapsed. The crew onboard the aircraft left, and finding the plane empty of pilots, the terrorists concluded that they had been tricked. A chaotic shootout ensued, killing the nine Israelis. They had been taken on two helicopters to the airport. In one helicopter the victims were shot to death. In the other the victims, who had been tied to their seats, died in a grenade blast. Although initial reports were sketchy, with some indicating that the Israelis had survived, ABC sportscaster Jim McKay announced to his global audience late in the evening that all the hostages had died. Five of the terrorists were also killed, as was one West German policeman. Three members of Black September were taken prisoner.

Israel's revenge for the Munich massacre was swift and cold-blooded, setting a model for dealing with terrorists in the future. PLO camps were targeted for bombings, and by most accounts (although Israel does not officially acknowledge this) special units of operatives were given the task of tracking down those connected to the attack, assassinating them one by one. The targets included the three Black September survivors of the airport shootout, who eventually were released by the West Germans after a mysterious airplane hijacking. One survivor eluded the Israelis and continues to live in hiding in 2012.

The Munich attack made it clear that large events such as the Olympics are not immune from terrorist attacks, and the result has been ever-greater security measures at such events. For the 2012 Summer Olympics in London security was elaborate, and some officials even proposed the placement of officers armed with missiles in residential areas. The September 11, 2001, attacks in New York City only reinforced, to many minds, the need for extensive security and constant diligence.

Meanwhile, athletic competition at Munich in 1972 was suspended on September 6, the day after the attack. That day a memorial ceremony was held in Munich's

Olympic Stadium and attended by eighty thousand people. There, the International Olympic Committee's chairman, Avery Brundage, announced that the games would continue, a decision that surprised many observers and, indeed, some of the athletes awaiting their events. The Munich games ended with a rather subdued closing ceremony on September 10.

Surviving Israeli athletes attended the memorial ceremony, but by then it already had been decided that they should abandon the games and leave Munich out of concern for new attacks. They flew back to Israel on the same airplane carrying the coffins of the eleven who had been killed. Among those in the coffins was David Berger, whose body eventually was brought back to the United States on a special US Air Force mission. His parents continue to mourn, as do survivors and family members of the other victims of the Munich Olympics massacre

World Map

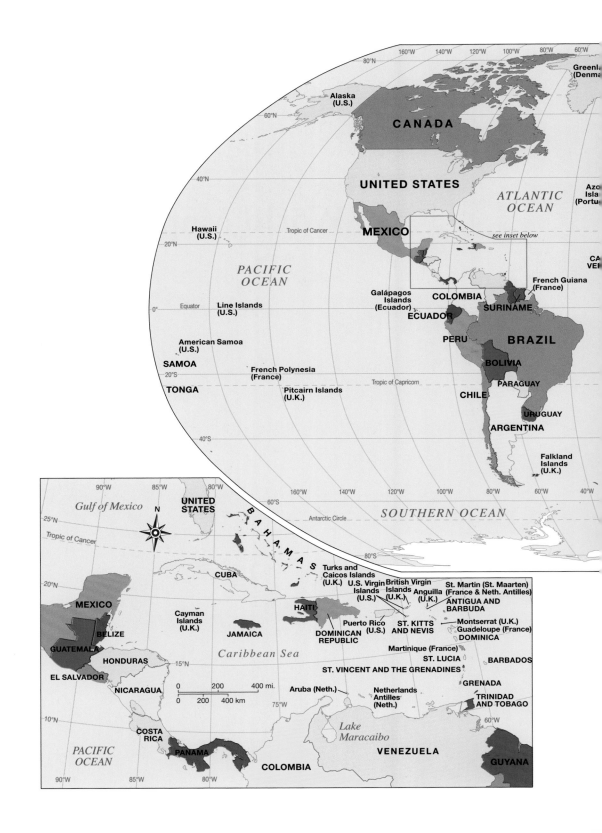

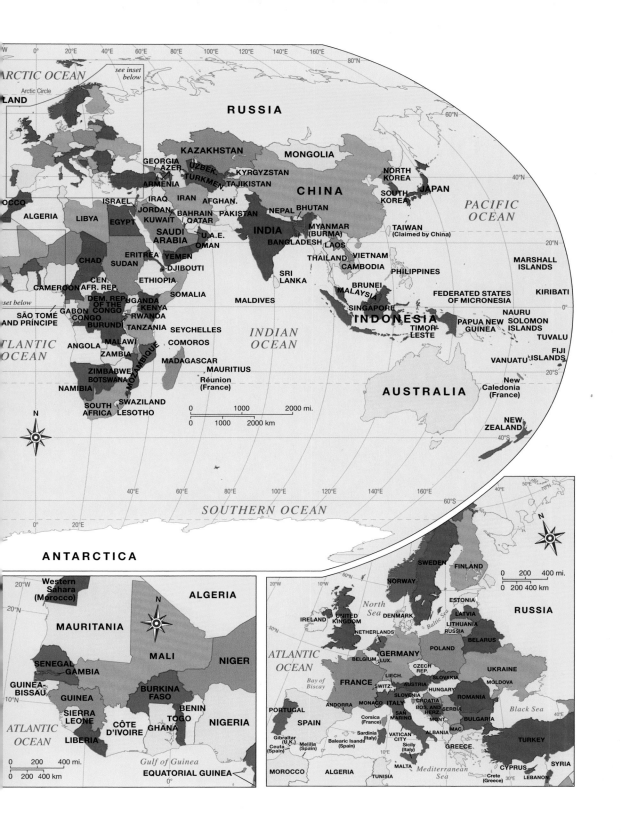

CHAPTER **1**

Historical Background on the Munich Olympics Massacre

The Events and Legacy of the Munich Olympics Massacre

Lisa Magloff

The 1972 Summer Olympics were held in Munich, a city in what was known as West Germany before the nation was reunited in 1990. It was the first time the Olympics had taken place on German soil since 1936 when they were staged in Berlin, the capital of what at that time was Adolf Hitler's Nazi Germany. In 1972 West Germany's democratic leaders, as well as the International Olympic Committee, wanted to present an event that was open, friendly, and marked by strong competition and good sportsmanship. Instead the games became the site of one of the most infamous terrorist attacks of the twentieth century.

In the following viewpoint, author Lisa Magloff describes how eight Palestinian terrorists, members of a group that called itself Black September, entered the athletes' village in Munich on

Photo on previous page: The Israeli delegation enters the Olympic Stadium in Munich, Germany, during the 1972 opening ceremonies. (© **Keystone-France/ Gamma-Keystone/Getty Images.**)

September 5, 1972. They then proceeded to take hostages, including members of Israel's Olympic delegation, hoping to exchange them for Palestinians held in Israeli prisons. The incident, as Magloff describes, went wrong and resulted in the deaths of eleven Israelis, one West German policeman, and five terrorists. The viewpoint also examines Israel's response to the attacks as well as other long-term effects of the attack. Magloff is the author of many educational and children's books.

Before the 1972 Munich Olympics, security for major international events was often lax, and terrorism was generally not a major concern among civilians. Much of this changed in 1972, when a group of Palestinian terrorists kidnapped nine Israeli athletes at the Olympic Games in Munich, Germany.

The hostage drama, which resulted in the death of 11 athletes, took place almost entirely under the glare of the media cameras. The world watched, horrified, as terrorism was brought into their homes for the first time. Neither security considerations, media coverage of terrorist incidents, nor the way the Western world views terrorism, has ever been the same since.

The Beginning

At around 5:00 A.M. on September 5, 1972, five terrorists hopped over the six-foot, six-inch fence surrounding the Olympic Village in Munich. Although they were seen by several people, athletes routinely hopped the fence, and no one thought it was odd. Once inside, they were met by three more terrorists who had obtained credentials to enter the village.

The terrorists first knocked on the door of the 33-year-old Israeli wrestling coach Moshe Weinberg. Weinberg opened the door, saw the attackers and shouted, "Boys, get out!" He and weightlifter Joseph Romano attempted to block the door while other Israeli athletes escaped. The terrorists fired through the door, mortally wounding Weinberg and killing Romano.

The noise of the shots alerted the Olympic Village to news of the attack. Although some Israeli athletes escaped by climbing out windows, the terrorists managed to capture nine more people before armed German police officers sealed off the area. Once the siege began, the terrorists announced that they were members of a Palestinian terrorist organization called Black September. At 9:35 A.M. the terrorists issued their demands. They set a noon deadline for the release of 200 Arab prisoners being held in Israeli jails, and they demanded safe passage out of Germany. They threatened to begin killing the athletes if their demands were not met.

> "The noise of the shots alerted the Olympic Village."

Negotiations dragged on for hours as the deadline was set back to 1 P.M., then 3 P.M., then 5 P.M., and finally cancelled. During the standoff, a great number of people became involved in the negotiations, including A.D. Tuney, the Egyptian mayor of the Olympic Village. The West German chancellor, Willy Brandt, consulted by phone with Prime Minister Golda Meir of Israel. The Israeli government announced that it would stand by its policy of never dealing with terrorists and would not negotiate. At 9 P.M., Brandt phoned President Anwar Sadat of Egypt. The Egyptian prime minister, Aziz Sidky, took the call, told Brandt, "We don't want to get involved in this," and hung up.

The Germans decided that the terrorists would kill their hostages if their demands were not met, so the decision was made to allow the terrorists to leave West Germany in exchange for the hostages' release. Meanwhile, Avery Brundage, the president of the International Olympic Committee, decided to allow the Games to continue during the siege. The public could watch the

The Modern State of Israel

In all, the Israeli Olympic delegation at the 1972 Munich Games consisted of only thirty people, fifteen of whom were competitive athletes. It was a small contingent from what, at that time, was a small nation only then in the process of becoming a regional power.

Modern Israel was born in 1948, with its first borders fully in place by 1949. Israel's founding was due to the efforts of European Jewish activists, or "Zionists," who had been establishing Jewish settlements in the region since the early 1900s. This settlement activity began under the Turkish Ottoman

Empire, which controlled Palestine until 1918, and then afterwards, when it was known as the British Palestinian Mandate.

The immigration of European Jews to the Mandate increased in the 1930s as thousands sought to escape Adolf Hitler's Nazi Germany. After World War II ended in 1945, with some six million Jews murdered by Hitler's regime, the migration to Palestine sped up even more despite British attempts to stop it because of violence between Jews and Palestinian Arabs. In 1947 the British announced that they were leaving Palestine, hope-

hostage drama unfolding on one TV channel, while athletes competed on another.

The Air Field Disaster

Although several plans were proposed, terrorists and police eventually agreed to a plan whereby the terrorists would be flown by helicopter to the military airbase at Fürstenfeldbruck, 15 miles away. There they would be met by a Lufthansa 737. The Tunisian government agreed to let a plane carrying the hostages and terrorists fly to Tunisia. Once in Tunisia, the hostages would be let go. West German negotiators would accompany the terrorists to the airfield to ensure their safety. Shortly after 10 P.M., the terrorists and hostages, followed by hundreds of media cameras, emerged from the building and walked to the helicopters. The Israeli hostages were

fully in the form of two states. But when Palestinian leaders refused to accept the proposed borders, Israeli Jews proceeded on their own to declare national independence. The new country was granted official recognition by the United Nations in January, 1948, and later that year the Israeli army defeated a coalition of Arab nations in the first Arab-Israeli War.

Israel remained small, poor, and largely ignored outside the region until the Six Day War in 1967. This conflict resulted in a decisive Israeli victory over a new Arab coalition as well as a vast expansion of the nation's borders.

Israel's successes showed that the new nation was well able to protect itself and that, despite the boasts of Arab leaders, it could not be "pushed into the sea." Friendships between Israel and other nations, such as the United States, began to flourish, and both foreign investment and new immigrants began to flow into the country. Among the newcomers were two athletes ready to compete under the Israeli banner at Munich: American-born weightlifter David Berger and Ukrainian-born wrestler Mark Slavin. Both died in the Munich massacre.

bound, blindfolded and tied close together. The German counterterrorist team had not dealt with such well-trained terrorists before and were not prepared. The German snipers had no radios with which to communicate with each other, and no night-vision goggles to help them see at night. This failure was to lead to disaster.

The German helicopter pilots had been told the police would try to rescue the Israelis once they had landed at the airbase, but after landing the terrorists told the pilots to stand in front of their aircraft, breaking an earlier promise that West Germans would not be involved as hostages. Two terrorists then walked the 170 yards to the plane for an inspection, bringing two hostages with them. As they were returning to the helicopters, German sharpshooters opened fire. In the ensuing firefight, the two terrorists and their hostages were killed. The remaining terrorists leaped from the helicopters, then turned and fired into one helicopter and tossed a hand grenade into the second, killing all of the hostages. The firefight continued, but with the hostages dead, the police did not hold back, and it was all over in a few minutes. In all, 11 athletes, 5 terrorists and 1 policeman were killed. Three of the terrorists were captured.

> The story of the Munich massacre continued for another 30 years, and its impact continues today.

Despite much criticism, Brundage decided to go ahead with the Games. The remaining 11 members of the Israeli team, however, did not stay for the end of the Games.

The Aftermath

Although the 1972 Olympic Games ended, the story of the Munich massacre continued for another 30 years, and its impact continues today. On October 29, 1972, just over a month after the Games, a Lufthansa jet was hijacked by Palestinian terrorists demanding the release of the three captured Munich terrorists. The Germans capitulated, and the terrorists were released.

Prime Minister Golda Meir of Israel then gave instructions for Israeli agents to hunt down and kill all those responsible for the Munich massacre. She told the Israeli Knesset on September 12, "We have no choice but to strike at the terrorist organizations wherever we can reach them. That is our obligation to ourselves and to peace. We shall fulfill that obligation undauntedly." At least eight Palestinian terrorists connected with Munich were assassinated in the following months, including the three released by West Germany.

In 1999, Abu Daoud, a member of the Palestine National Council, admitted in his autobiography, *Palestine: From Jerusalem to Munich*, that he had been responsible for planning the Munich operation. Daoud (whose real

name is Mohammed Daoud Machmoud Auda) had earlier admitted that Black September was a cover for Fatah, Yasir Arafat's faction of the Palestine Liberation Organization (PLO). Daoud wrote in his autobiography that he had briefed Arafat before the attack, and Arafat had sent him off on the mission with the words, "Allah protect you." Daoud wrote that he had no regrets over the deaths, but did regret that instead of rousing sympathy for the PLO cause, they caused only revulsion.

Besides Daoud, at least one other PLO terrorist linked to the Munich attack was given a position in the Palestinian Authority (PA)—Amin al Hindi, who headed Arafat's General Intelligence Service. Israel objected in 1995 when Arafat tried to appoint another Munich suspect, Mustafa Liftawi (Abu Firas), as PA police chief in Ramallah.

An armed police officer in a track suit scales and enters the Olympic Village building where Israeli athletes are being held hostage on September 5, 1972. (© Hulton Archive/Getty Images.)

The families of the victims were initially paid $1 million in compensation by the German government, but they later sued, saying that the German police had bungled the rescue attempt by stationing only five poorly equipped snipers at the airfield. The German government has always denied responsibility for the deaths, arguing that they had done everything they could, and the lawsuit brought by the families was rejected by several German courts, most recently in 1999.

The Munich Olympics marked the end of naivete in planning security for large, international proceedings. Never again would police find themselves so unequipped or have such a lax attitude about security precautions for major events. Watching the events on TV also brought terrorism that much closer to home for many ordinary people, creating, for the first time, an awareness of the price paid for poor planning and inadequate protection.

Terrorists Turn '72 Munich Olympics Into Bloodbath

Bruce Lowitt

In the following selection, reporter Bruce Lowitt provides a step-by-step narrative of the events of September 5, 1972, the day of the Munich Olympics massacre. He traces the events from the arrival of Palestinian terrorists in the Olympic Village early in the morning to that evening's shootout near the Fürstenfeldbruck airfield, a military base outside Munich. Along the way he touches on the shooting of two Israelis inside their compound, the protracted negotiations that followed, and the involvement of high-level politicians and officials. Lowitt also comments on some events that followed, including a surprising decision to continue the games.

SOURCE. Bruce Lowitt, "Terrorists Turn '72 Olympics into Bloodbath," *St. Petersburg Times,* December 29, 1999. Copyright © 1999 by Tampa Bay Times. All rights reserved. Reproduced by permission.

Time was, wars were suspended during the Olympics and armies prohibited from attacking the ancient Games. Truces permitted worshippers and athletes to travel safely.

Times change.

Modern Olympics have been suspended for two world wars.

At 4:30 A.M. Sept. 5, 1972, war, politics and religion invaded the Munich Olympics.

Terrorists claiming to be from Black September, a Palestinian guerrilla group, stole into the Olympic Village dressed as athletes and carrying their weapons in gym bags. They killed two Israelis and took nine hostage.

The terrorists demanded the release of 200 Arab guerrillas jailed in Israel and safe passage for themselves and the hostages. By 11 P.M. the hostages, five of their captors and one West German police officer were dead, the outcome of a failed rescue attempt. Three Arabs were captured.

> During the siege, with two Israelis already dead, Avery Brundage, president of the International Olympic Committee, ordered that the Games continue:

During the siege, with two Israelis already dead, Avery Brundage, president of the International Olympic Committee, ordered that the Games continue.

"Walled off in their dream world," *New York Times* columnist Red Smith wrote, "appallingly unaware of the realities of life and death, the aging playground directors who conduct this quadrennial muscle dance ruled that a little blood must not be permitted to interrupt play."

The following day, competition was suspended. The 11 surviving Israeli Olympians, wearing white yarmulkes and maroon blazers, sat among 3,000 athletes, surrounded by 80,000 spectators, honoring and mourning their murdered teammates in a memorial service at the enormous Olympic Stadium.

VICTIMS OF THE MUNICH OLYMPIC MASSACRE

Name	Affiliation	Cause of Death	Location
David Berger	Israeli weight-lifting team	Grenade blast	Helicopter at airport
Ze'ev Friedman	Israeli weight-lifting team	Grenade blast	Helicopter at airport
Yosef Gutfreund	Israeli wrestling referee	Shot	Helicopter at airport
Eliezer Halfin	Israeli wrestling team	Grenade blast	Helicopter at airport
Yossef Romano	Israeli wrestling team	Shot	Olympic Village
Amitzur Shapira	Israeli track coach	Shot	Helicopter at airport
Kehat Shorr	Israeli shooting coach	Shot	Helicopter at airport
Mark Slavin	Israeli wrestling team	Shot	Helicopter at airport
Andre Spitzer	Israeli fencing coach	Shot	Helicopter at airport
Yakov Springer	Israeli weight-lifting judge	Grenade blast	Helicopter at airport
Moshe Weinberg	Israeli wrestling coach	Shot	Olympic Village
Anton Fliegerbauer	German police officer	Shot	Airport
Luttif Afif	Black September	Shot	Airport
Afif Ahmed Hamid	Black September	Shot	Airport
Khalid Jawad	Black September	Shot	Airport
Yusuf Nazzal	Black September	Shot	Airport
Ahmed Chic Thaa	Black September	Shot	Airport

Five hours later, Brundage decreed that the Games resume, another controversial decision criticized by Israel and other nations, though some Israelis said canceling the Games would have been giving in to blackmail. Also controversial: a pre-Olympic decision by Israel to deal with its security concerns without special treatment from West Germany.

From various accounts, this is what took place that Tuesday in September:

The assault on 31 Connolly St., one of the buildings at the Olympic Village, began at about 5 A.M. with a knock on the door of 33-year-old wrestling coach Moshe Weinberg. He opened it a crack, saw the attackers, put his shoulder to the door and shouted, "Boys, get out!" Weightlifting coach Tuvia Sokolsky said that as he fled, he saw Weinberg hit by a hail of bullets through the door.

Weinberg was ordered to lead the terrorists to other Israeli rooms. He pointed to one with wrestlers and weightlifters, hoping they could overpower the attackers. Then he collapsed and died.

Joseph Romano, 32, a weightlifter, was next to die, also by automatic rifle fire. By now, other Israelis were being warned of the attack. Six escaped through a rear door. Three hundred armed police officers sealed off the area. Brundage and other Olympic officials convened. The siege began.

At 9:35 A.M. the terrorists issued their demands. Negotiations with Munich police chief Manfred Schreiber, in charge of Olympic security, commenced. The Arabs set a noon deadline. They said two Israelis would be shot if the demands were not met.

The deadline was set back to 1 P.M., then 3, then 5, then the Arabs canceled it. Negotiations dragged on. The terrorists rejected an offer of unlimited ransom. They rejected an offer by Schreiber that he and two high-ranking officials take the hostages' place. In Israel, Premier Golda

Photo on previous page: Athletes and other spectators watch from nearby fields and buildings as the hostage crisis unfolds in Munich's Olympic Village on September 5, 1972. (© Guido Cegani; Mario De Biasi; Sergio Del Grande; Giorgio Lotti; Walter Mori; Giuseppe Pino/Mondadori Portfolio/Getty Images.)

Palestinian Refugees

Black September terrorists launched their attack on the Munich Olympics hoping to bring the world's attention to what seemed to them to be a forgotten cause: that of Palestinian Arab refugees.

The issue of Palestinian refugees arose in 1948 and 1949, when the modern state of Israel was created. As borders were drawn, many Palestinians found themselves uprooted or, alternatively, unwelcomed in the new state. Many more thousands of Palestinian refugees were created after the Arab-Israeli Six Day War of 1967. Then, Israel defeated a coalition of Arab countries and, in the process, greatly expand-

ed their country's borders. Among the places that Israel took possession of in 1967 was the West Bank of the Jordan River, largely inhabited by Palestinians, as well as East, or "Old" Jerusalem, up to then a region managed politically by the neighboring Kingdom of Jordan. Newly homeless Palestinians often found themselves facing uncertain futures in refugee camps in Israel, Jordan, Lebanon, or Syria.

Israel's Arab neighbors were hesitant to accept large numbers of Palestinians as permanent residents, although they often used these refugees as a political tool. The Palestine Liberation Organization (PLO), a poten-

Meir said her government stood by its policy of not dealing with terrorists.

Schreiber said he believed the building could not be successfully stormed, that the terrorists were desperate and would not relent no matter how many lives were lost. He and his colleagues spent the afternoon devising plans to get the Arabs and Israelis out. At dusk, the terrorists said they would consider leaving with the hostages.

Negotiators began trying to persuade the terrorists they could leave West Germany safely. But they were working under Brundage's instructions not to let the Arabs leave with the hostages.

A helicopter pad was hastily built nearby. The Tunisian ambassador obtained permission from his govern-

tial leadership group, was founded in 1964 but was not very active until after the Six Day War. By then, leaders such as Yasser Arafat understood that they could hope for little support from their Arab "sponsors" and needed to act on their own behalf. Some PLO members, including those connected to the radical Fatah faction, were ready to use terrorist tactics such as kidnappings, assassinations, and airplane hijackings. These were already being used or considered by radical organizations in Europe such as West Germany's Baader-Meinhof Group and Italy's Red Brigade. Palestinian terrorists continued to mount attacks through much of the 1970s and 1980s, using them generally to maintain the world's attention on the lives of Palestinian refugees.

In the 1990s and 2000s, and despite continued violence, the PLO was slowly displaced by a Palestinian Authority designed to provide government to certain areas inhabited by Palestinians such as the Gaza Strip and the West Bank city of Ramallah. Indeed, Palestinian status was secure enough that, in 1996, it sent its first team to an Olympic Games. Still, hundreds of thousands of Palestinian refugees remain in camps waiting for the creation of a full Palestinian state or a return to homes they claim to have lost.

ment to let a plane carrying the hostages and terrorists land at a Tunisian airfield.

At 8 P.M. a bus pulled up to 31 Connolly St. The Arab leader demanded a different green army bus "so there was no chance to do anything," Schreiber said later. "They were too clever."

At 8:50 P.M. the first of three helicopters landed at the Olympic Village. Meanwhile, a Lufthansa 737 was flown to the military air base at Fürstenfeldbruck, 15 miles west of the village.

At 9 P.M. West German Chancellor Willy Brandt phoned President Anwar el-Sadat of Egypt. Premier Aziz Sidky reportedly took the call and, when asked for help, told Brandt, "We do not want to get involved in this" and hung up.

A minute or two after 10 P.M., the terrorists and hostages emerged from the building, the Israelis bound, blindfolded and tied close together. "This made it impossible to try anything with sharpshooters inside the village," Schreiber recalled. Weightlifters David Berger, 26, and Zeev Friedman, 28; weightlifting instructor Yacob Springer, 51; wrestlers Eliezer Halfin, 28, and Mark Slavin, 18; wrestling referee Yosef Gutfreund, 41; fencing coach Andre Spitzer, 45; athletics coach Amitzur Shapira, 32, and marksmanship coach Kehat Schorr, 53, were herded into the bus. Schreiber and two officials rode with them to the helicopters. The West Germans boarded one, the terrorists and hostages the others. They landed at Fürstenfeldbruck at 10:30 P.M.

The pilots had been told the West Germans would try to rescue the Israelis because allowing the Arabs to leave with them "would have been a certain death sentence for the hostages," Bruno Merk, interior minister of Bavaria, said. What happened was not what the pilots expected. The Arabs told them to stand in front of their aircraft, breaking a promise that West Germans would not be involved as hostages. Two Arabs and one or more Israelis walked the 170 yards to the plane for an inspection. They were walking back when one or more sharpshooters hidden in the darkness fired. In the ensuing firefight, the Arabs on the ground killed the Israelis with them. Other terrorists leaped from the helicopters. Several unleashed automatic fire into one, killing the Israelis inside. One of the terrorists tossed a hand grenade into the other helicopter, killing its occupants.

Five days later, in the rain, a subdued closing ceremony was held that included a silent meditation and fewer athletes than usual. The flags of the competing nations were paraded around the stadium. Israel's was not among them.

Broadcasting the Events of Munich in Real Time

Tom Hoffarth

ABC Sports sent a large team of journalists and technicians to cover the Munich Olympics for the US television market. Among them were Jim McKay, a widely respected sports journalist who hosted the popular weekly program ABC's *Wide World of Sports;* Peter Jennings, the later anchor of ABC's *Evening News,* who happened to be in town; and Howard Cosell, best remembered for his blunt viewpoints on *Monday Night Football*. The ABC team was equipped with the latest in satellite TV technology, a new method at the time that made it easy to beam the Olympics to audiences at the same time the events were taking place. When Palestinian terrorists attacked the Israeli Olympic delegation in Munich, McKay and the rest of the ABC team found themselves reporters of political events, not sports.

In the following viewpoint, Los Angeles reporter Tom Hoffarth writes of Jim McKay's memories of the attack. McKay (who passed away in 2008) stayed on air for some fifteen hours on September 5, 1972, the day of the attack. It fell to him to announce to audiences

---

in the United States—and elsewhere around the world—that all the hostages had been killed.

Suppose, says Jim McKay, you were tuning in to watch a World Series.

"In the fourth inning, terrorists appear on the field, take all the players in the dugout hostage and hold them there for hours," the legendary ABC sportscaster continues.

Doesn't matter what channel you're watching at this point. Every network has broken in with live coverage. "A helicopter comes to scoop them up and take them to the airport," McKay continues. "But gunfire breaks out and they're all killed."

As horrific as that would be—it would be more believable as a movie than in real life—suppose that incident wasn't even the worst act of terrorism ever to have affected a sporting event.

Try as he might with that World Series scenario, McKay knows nothing can really compare to what he reported on live 25 years ago today.

On September 5, 1972—the 10th day of the two-week Summer Olympics in Munich, West Germany—eight Arab guerrillas with submachine guns and ski masks climbed over an unguarded back fence and burst into the Israeli living quarters at Building 31. Two Israelis were killed at first, and nine hostages eventually died in a botched rescue attempt. Five terrorists and one German policeman also died in the episode.

For 16 hours, McKay anchored ABC's coverage from a small TV studio just yards from where the hostage siege began. He had been at countless Olympic Games as host and reporter, won two sports Emmys for his work, had seen all the proverbial human drama of athletic competition as the original host on ABC's *Wide World of Sports* for more than a decade.

But this would be the defining moment in his broadcast career. From his home in Maryland, McKay says it's "extraordinary that people talk about it on a regular basis . . . at least two or three times a month I'll be stopped somewhere, say the supermarket, and instead of talking about something that happened last week, they want to talk about Munich."

Newspeople and Sportscasters

It may be unfair to ask someone to remember details from something that happened a quarter-century ago. But McKay remembers it all too well.

Asleep in his hotel room with his wife, he was awakened by a call from ABC Sports executive Roone Arledge to help cover an event that was about as distant from an athletic contest as one could imagine.

Chris Schenkel, ABC's prime-time host, had just left the TV chair hours before and gone to bed. Peter Jennings, then ABC's Middle East field correspondent "on vacation" in Munich, wasn't well known enough. McKay was ABC's play-by-play man on gymnastics, which had just ended, and he was about to do the track and field.

"I asked Roone, 'Why me?'" McKay recalled. "Roone told me that he never thought of me as a sportscaster but more of as a reporter. And this was a reporter's event."

> The image of McKay in his yellow ABC blazer is etched into so many viewers' minds.

Working with only one static camera shot of the terrorists just outside the broadcast complex—and not oblivious to the fact the TV studio could be taken over as well—McKay went on with a telecast that could have turned at any moment and in any direction.

The image of McKay in his yellow ABC blazer is etched into so many viewers' minds, as are the words he spoke—"They're all gone"—when the deaths were

The Munich police chief answers questions at a press conference during the hostage crisis. Media coverage was non-stop throughout the day. (© **AP Photo.**)

confirmed. It wasn't until about six months ago [in 1997], when McKay started writing his autobiography and was asked to do a voice-over of that scene for a movie on [Olympic runner] Steve Prefontaine, that he finally saw the tape of his reporting on that day.

"I tried to relive it as I watched, but the one thing I couldn't feel again was the exhaustion," he said. "I couldn't look at all 16 hours, but I can't believe I really talked that long.

"I also couldn't believe all we had was one camera, wheeled out to this little knoll right near the fence. It was 25 yards to the fence and another 75 to Building 31. And that's exact. I paced it off a year later when I was back there."

Hour after hour, the broadcast continued. McKay said he had no trouble keeping focused. "The one thing

I remembered all day was this young weightlifter named David Berger, who was on the Israel team but was from Shaker Heights, Ohio. I knew I'd be the only one who could tell the family about the fate of their son. That really does help you keep things on the road to accuracy." Especially when German TV continued to broadcast false reports about the athletes' safety.

The one hour ABC had to get off the air—CBS had booked the satellite time and wouldn't give it up—McKay continued on radio.

"Many people were surprised that I was in that seat and I could do the job," he said. "But reporting is reporting. The techniques are the same as in a sporting event.

"With only one camera on a suite of rooms watching people going in and out, it was incredible mystery. The emotions were intense, wondering who was dead and who was alive. It had all the elements."

Mixed Reports

McKay remembers after it all ended returning to a hotel room that "was all dark and quiet. My wife was asleep, and she woke up and said, 'Well, at least they're all safe.' She had heard the reports on the German TV. I had to tell her, 'No, all of them were killed.'

"I really didn't lie awake thinking about it because I had to get up in three hours for a memorial service, which was scheduled on the first day of the decathlon. You wouldn't believe how many spectators went to bed like my wife thinking everyone was saved. They were mystified when they came to the stadium the next day and didn't know what was going on."

And McKay believes, as many others still do, that the Games resumed much too soon after what had just happened. At the memorial service, IOC [International Olympic Committee] chief Avery Brundage gave what McKay called "amounted to a political speech for the Olympics" to not cave into terrorism and move forward.

"It was so bizarre to look through the glass to the control room where we had 20 to 30 monitors and here's the dressage going on one place, and boxing going on over there," McKay said. "I kept thinking, 'That's a different world, eons away.' To pick up the next day seemed callous to me."

Some tried to compare Munich to the events last year at the [1996] Atlanta Games, when a bomb exploded in Olympic Park and caused one death. McKay, in Atlanta as a corporate host for Delta Airlines when that occurred, says the tragedies 24 years and six Olympiads apart have few similarities. World events and the political climate were much different. For one, West Germany doesn't exist today.

"What happened in Atlanta was very different," said McKay, who didn't see any of NBC's coverage of that episode. "For one, it was a domestic event. It had an impact on the games, but not as much as it did in Munich.

"We weren't used to those kind of things happening at that time, especially in the greatest peaceful gathering of man every four years. On that occasion, it struck everyone in the heart around the world."

The deadline is the end of October for McKay to finish his autobiography, tentatively titled *Around the World in 50 Years,* which is how long he's been a sportscaster.

It wasn't tough selecting what point to start the book.

"My editor told me the first chapter had to be the Munich Games," McKay said. "I guess that makes sense. It's what everyone remembers me for."

Olympics Memorial for Eleven Israeli Athletes

Nissan Ratzlav-Katz

Ever since the Munich attack, survivors and family members of the victims have tried to convince Olympic officials that a memorial event should be staged at every subsequent summer games. Among the most active of these lobbyists has been Ankie Spitzer, whose husband Andre Spitzer was one of those killed, and Ilana Romano, widow of wrestler Yosef (Yossi) Romano. For their part, Olympic officials have consistently refused to stage such a memorial, citing their contention that, as much as possible, politics should be kept separate from sports.

Despite the opinions of Olympic officials, Israelis have held commemorations of their own. In the following viewpoint, Israeli writer Nissan Ratzlav-Katz describes the memorial that took place at the 2008 Summer Olympics in Beijing, China. Among those who attended were current and former members of the International Olympic Committee, including a German representative, and the Israeli ambassador to China. For the 2012 summer games in London, Israelis planned a similar ceremony after receiving official word that, once again, there would be no large-scale commemoration involving the entire Olympic community.

A ceremony in memory of the 11 Israeli athletes murdered by PLO terrorists during the 1972 Munich Olympics was held Monday evening in Beijing's Olympic Village. As in past years, the Israeli Olympic Committee and the Israeli Foreign Ministry arranged the memorial on their own.

Hundreds of people attended the event, held at the Hilton hotel in Beijing, including foreign diplomats and Olympic representatives. Taking part in the memorial from Israel were Minister of Science, Culture and Sport Ghaleb Majadele, members of the current Israeli Olympic delegation and the Israeli Olympic Committee, Israel's representative to the International Olympic Committee (IOC), and ambassador to China Amos Nadai.

Among the IOC representatives in attendance were the head of the German Olympic Committee, Thomas Bach, and former IOC President Juan Antonio Samaranch, as well as a number of Olympic delegates from other nations. Current IOC president Jacques Rogge was in Hong Kong on Monday and unable to attend the Beijing event.

> "Israel's next memorial ceremony for the 1972 Olympic delegation should be held 'under the Olympics' five-ring banner.

On September [5], 1972, a Fatah terrorist front group going under the name of Black September infiltrated the Olympic Village in Germany and took 11 Israeli athletes hostage. After negotiations, a botched rescue attempt led to the deaths of the bound Israeli captives. The mastermind of the Munich attack, Mohammed Daoud Oudeh, or Abu Daoud, revealed in a 1999 memoir that current Palestinian Authority Chairman and Fatah leader Mahmoud Abbas handled the financing for the Munich attack.

Since the 1976 Montreal Olympics, the Israeli delegation to the Games has held a memorial for the fallen athletes. The IOC has yet to take part in sponsoring the event or in officially marking the anniversary of the attacks in any way.

"We should have had his memorial in front of all the athletes, sponsored by the IOC," said Ankie Spitzer, widow of fencing coach Andre Spitzer. 'This is not an Israeli issue. This concerns the whole Olympic family."

The widow of weightlifter Yosef Romano, Ilana, called on the IOC to "recognize those murdered as sons of the Olympic movement." Israel's next memorial ceremony for the 1972 Olympic delegation should be held "under the Olympics' five-ring banner," Romano said.

Ilana Romano (left) and Ankie Spitzer—widows of Israeli athletes killed during the Munich Olympics Massacre— continue to petition the International Olympic committee for a public minute of silence during the Games. They are pictured here in 2012 at the London Olympics. (© AP Photo/ Lefteris Pitarakis.)

In her words to the assembled IOC delegates, Spitzer commented that "nations that are not willing to condemn terrorism openly or refuse to compete against other nations because of their nationality or race or religion—they should not be part of the Olympics. It's contrary to the Olympic ideal."

In a brief speech, Samaranch called the Munich Massacre, as it came to be known, "the blackest event in the long history of the Olympic Games." The murder of 11 "athletes, coaches and judges of your country who came to the Olympic Games to compete in peace and harmony" was "an event that the world and the Olympic movement will never forget," he said.

"We will not allow terror to triumph," declared Israel Olympic Committee President Zvi Varshaviak, adding that the attack was targeted at Israelis, but all Olympic athletes "continue their path" by continuing to take part in the Games.

Munich 1972: When Terrorism "Contaminated" the Olympics

Kelly Whiteside

In the following viewpoint, Avraham Melamed, a swimmer on Israel's 1972 Olympic team, offers his perspective on the Munich massacre at a distance of forty years. His interviewer, journalist Kelly Whiteside, provides the unique perspective of one of the eleven Israeli athletes who survived the attack. The viewpoint notes how security in the Olympic Village was fairly relaxed; Melamed was lucky to be staying in the building that the terrorists chose not to storm. Along the way Whiteside tells Melamad's story of training in the United States and, after the attack, going to live there permanently. She also notes how Melamed is joining other survivors in the production of a documentary on the massacre.

A thin wall separated victim from survivor when Palestinian terrorists stormed the Olympic Village in Munich on Sept. 5, 1972. The terrorists took their first hostages—a group of Israeli coaches and officials in Apartment 1—then moved on to Apartment 3, which housed Israeli weightlifters and wrestlers. Those in Apartment 2 were spared.

Forty years after 11 Israeli Olympians were killed in Munich, a thin wall still separates the beauty of the Games from the horror of that day, especially for Avraham Melamed, who was sleeping that night in Apartment 2.

"The Olympics were a virgin phenomenon," says Melamed, a two-time Olympic swimmer for Israel. "It's not a virgin anymore. Now you have to think about security. Now you have to think about terrorism. Now you have to plan for it. It comes at an enormous price. And this beautiful thing that's supposed to symbolize forgetting about politics, forgetting about war, for this period of time ... now it's contaminated. Now it's contaminated forever."

> The attack was a pivotal event in the evolution of global terrorism and the reason security for the Olympics has increased dramatically.

Still, this summer he will watch, intently as always, when the Olympics are held in London from July 27 to Aug. 12. "I sit mesmerized by the television," says Melamed, 67.

What he will see is an Olympics much changed since the Munich massacre. The attack was a pivotal event in the evolution of global terrorism and the reason security for the Olympics has increased dramatically. The Munich Games employed 2,140 police and other law enforcement officers, according to the official report, Olympic historian David Wallechinsky said. The London Games will have a security force of 23,700, according to the British government's most recent report. With a security budget of at least $1.6 billion, the London Games are the largest peacetime security operation in Britain's history.

For London, there is plenty of reason for added vigilance. A day after the city was awarded the Games in 2005, suicide bombers attacked the city's transit system, killing 52 people. As a U.S. ally in Iraq and Afghanistan, Britain is also increasingly concerned about the threat from Islamic militants.

"A Little Bit Guilty"

Early on Saturday mornings, you can find Avraham Melamed, who is known as Bey, gliding across a modest pool at a health club about an hour north of New York City. Directly after the Munich Games, he flew to the USA to finish college and has lived here ever since. "I'm about 5-7, bald, aging and," he says by way of description, "better than your average recreational swimmer."

After his workout, the swimmers on the Premier Athletic Club masters team he coaches arrive for practice. Still wet, Melamed walks around the pool in bare feet, black swimming trunks and white T-shirt, coaxing and encouraging. Erika Krumlauf, 42, says she had no idea who Melamed was when she joined the team. After a quick Google search, she learned that he swam for Israel in the 1964 and 1968 Olympics. She later read that her coach survived the 1972 Munich massacre.

In February, Melamed told his swimmers he would miss practice because of a scheduled trip to Munich. "I asked him if it was for vacation," says Tom Seery, 51. "He said, 'Not really.'"

He didn't mention that he was returning to Munich for the first time in 40 years to be interviewed for the documentary *The Eleventh Day—The Survivors of Munich 1972*. The film, produced by the German Biography Channel in collaboration with the Israeli History Channel, will premiere on German television July 7, just ahead of the London Games.

Surviving members of the Israeli team hold their country's flag at a funeral ceremony for their killed teammates in Munich on September 6, 1972. (© Keystone-France/Gamma-Keystone/ Getty Images.)

Melamed still has mixed feelings about the attention. "I feel a little strange about sort of deriving notoriety from this incident. I feel a little bit guilty.

"My friends died," he says, rubbing his hand across his smooth head. "My friends died. I'm not a victim. I'm a survivor."

Melamed began swimming at a young age in Israel. He competed in the 1964 Toyko Games, failing to advance beyond the heats in the 200-meter butterfly. In the 1968 Games in Mexico City, he tied for 10th place in the 100 butterfly and 15th place in the 200.

After a chance meeting with a U.S. coach at the 1970 World University Games, Melamed headed to study in the USA and swim for West Liberty State College near Wheeling, W.Va. He encouraged three other Israel teammates to join him, and the Hilltoppers soon became an NAIA power. They were profiled in a lengthy feature in *Sports Illustrated* in 1972 titled, "Wandering Jews in an Unpromising Land." The piece took great delight in the incongruity. One passage, quoting Melamed, read: "'Coach described it as a small town. But a small town in the States, I thought, would be 100,000 people—50,000, at least.' What he (Melamed) found was a town of 500— 450 of whom must be in perpetual hiding."

Melamed was a three-time NAIA All-American and won five individual national championships during his three seasons, according to the West Liberty Hall of Fame.

Once-Lax Security

In part because he was training in the USA and mostly because of internal politics in Israeli swimming, Melamed was not named to the 1972 Olympic team. Given he was one of the country's top swimmers, there was an uproar. The controversy was chronicled in an Israeli newspaper, which sent Melamed to Munich as a reporter. However, he didn't have a news media credential and thus was not granted official access to Olympic facilities. But because he had begun serving as a personal coach for one of the team's female swimmers, he was invited by Israeli officials to stay with the team's delegation in the Village— which, in a tragic irony, he was able to do quite easily without a credential.

In 1972, Germany's goal was to distance itself from its last Olympics, the 1936 Nazi Games in Berlin. Security personnel wore turquoise uniforms and patrolled the Games unarmed during the day. (In London, as in recent Olympics, there will be strict security measures at the Village. Credentials will be checked repeatedly and belongings will be X-rayed on entry.)

Melamed recalls sneaking into the Munich Olympic Village as a matter of routine. "I didn't even have a key to the apartment," he says. "They say there was no security. The truth is that the people there did not have guns, but it was much better protected than Tokyo, where you could get everywhere, and in Mexico City, where you just had to pay a couple of pesos."

> Melamed recalls sneaking into the Munich Olympic village as a matter of routine.

The terrorists sneaked into the village with the ease of a kid who missed curfew. Wearing track suits and carrying duffel bags, they arrived in the middle of the night as some American athletes were returning from a night on the town. The two groups scaled the 6-foot fence together.

Before dawn, Melamed says he was awakened by a muffled shot and screams. "It sounded like someone in a room behind you kept their television loud and that there was a Western movie," he says.

In the next apartment, wrestling coach Moshe Weinberg had been shot in a struggle. When Melamed was a student at a teacher's college in Israel, Weinberg was the head of residences, and the two were friends. "It seemed so like a dream that doesn't make sense," Melamed says.

The terrorists, who were part of the Black September faction of the Palestine Liberation Organization, forced the badly wounded coach to lead them to the apartments where other Israelis were housed. Weinberg skipped Apartment 2, where Melamed and other slightly built residents were, and moved on to Apartment 3, where the wrestlers and weightlifters lived, presumably with the hope that the latter group could overpower the terrorists. The residents of Apartment 2 slipped out of the back sliding door to safety.

How the rest of the story unfolded has been told and retold in books, films and documentaries. After the Olympians were taken hostage, long hours of negotiations followed as the world watched—and the footage of a terrorist in a stocking cap became the Games' indelible image. The 11 Israelis were killed after a botched rescue attempt at a military airfield.

"They let us visit the room, where they kept our friends. All of their belongings were strewn, and there was a huge pool of blood. It was like a dream that you observe from the outside. You want to feel something, but all you feel is anger," Melamed says. "Rationally we knew that the Germans had zero interest in supporting anything like this. But the whole association of Jews getting killed again on German soil, there was a lot of anger."

> 'But [with] the whole association of Jews getting killed again on German soil, there was a lot of anger.'

"You Go On"

After the Games, Melamed returned to the USA, finished his undergraduate degree at West Liberty and went to graduate school at the University of Massachusetts, where he coached the men's swimming team from 1973 to 1979. "Being not in Israel helped me," he says. "I didn't feel like I became a different person, but my girlfriend at the time said I changed. The change was subtle; I don't know what it was. It's like people surviving a tornado. You go on. It was a tornado in my life. It was disruptive, but it passed."

Melamed went on. He became a computer science programmer in New York, married, started a family, divorced and continued to swim and coach the sport he loved. He didn't see or speak to any of the other survivors for 40 years, until he was contacted by the documentary filmmakers and asked to return to Munich. Seven survivors gathered on a chilly, rainy day. "It was good to hear their stories. Each one of us had slightly different perspectives. It was great to see them and the people they came to be," says Melamed, the only U.S.-based survivor.

Emanuel Rotstein, the director of production for the documentary, says no previous book or film has focused on the survivors. "It's almost unbelievable that those men who survived such a terrible assault on their lives disappeared from the collective memory and didn't play any role in the way the attacks were reported and even commemorated up to now," Rotstein says.

The group returned to their building in the Olympic Village, which is now a middle-class apartment complex. In front of Building 31, there is a memorial plaque. The building looks the same, but the surroundings aren't as stark, Melamed says. "Now there is a lot more flowers and plants. Time has taken its course and changed it," he says.

Those gathered asked if they could go into the apartment, but a woman living there refused.

"Our friends were very upset; I wasn't," Melamed says. "It was pretty ridiculous to expect them to know you, or to respect you. We were just intruders to them, all of a sudden, 15 people coming with cameras."

But the group didn't need to see the central scene of the tragedy to relive it. "I have memories, and they are fading as we speak," Melamed says with a small smile.

"Can you believe it's been 40 years since Munich?" he is asked.

"Do I have a choice? I can't believe I can't swim 200 butterfly anymore!" he says. "I can't believe this, I can't believe that, but I have to live."

CHAPTER 2

Controversies Surrounding the Munich Olympics Massacre

The Germans Wanted to Create a Relaxed, Friendly Environment for Olympic Athletes

Organizing Committee for the Games of the XXth Olympiad

In 1972, as a result of post–World War II events, Germany was divided into two nations. East Germany was allied with Communist Soviet Union. The Games were held in West Germany, or the Federal Republic of Germany, a democratic ally of the United States and other Western nations. Both German nations were sensitive about their fairly recent Nazi past. From 1933 to 1945 the country was controlled by Adolf Hitler's regime, which infamously targeted European Jews for extinction.

The 1972 Olympics were the first to be held on German soil since the so-called Nazi Olympics of 1936 in Berlin. West German organizers planned the event in ways they hoped would quell any

SOURCE. Organizing Committee for the Games of the XXth Olympiad, "Die Spiele: The Official Report," Munich, Germany, 1972. Copyright © 1972 by International Olympic Committee. All rights reserved. Reproduced with permission.

reminders of the Nazi era, putting unarmed guards in civilian clothes and otherwise creating an open, friendly environment. In the following viewpoint, taken from an official report issued after the massacre, West Germany's Olympic Organizing Committee describes their plans. Neither the Germans nor the Israeli representatives believed they had anything to fear regarding security at the Munich Olympic Village.

The Games of the XXth Olympiad should have proceeded in a serene, unconstrained and peaceful fashion. The architecture, the visual configuration and the organization expressed this idea. The security conception also had to adjust itself to this idea, although its planning provided that its effectiveness would not thereby be impaired. This was no place for an absolute priority to be given to every conceivable aspect of security or for a total presence of heavily armed police. Barbed wire and machine guns would not have been appropriate for the creation of a peaceful atmosphere of international encounter at the Olympic contests, nor could these give the world at large a true picture of the Federal Republic of Germany [West Germany]. Military uniforms were not desired; as opposed to this, the sport clothing worn by the surveillance personnel was to have created a cheerful climate and would have discreetly blended into the Olympic rainbow of color. The same concept was also valid for the Olympic Village. Its arrangement, security and accessibility fitted into the overall image of the Olympic facilities. These should be no enclosed fortress with walls, barbed wire and watchtowers. There had never been such a completely enclosed village at previous Olympic Games. Therefore, only a two-meter high wire-netting fence closed off the Olympic Village from the outside.

"A civil security service wearing friendly, light blue uniforms was created."

A civil security service wearing friendly, light blue uniforms was created. It was composed essentially of

Munich's Olympic Park, seen here in 1972, includes the Olympic Stadium (center) and the Olympiaturm, or Olympic Tower. Portions of the Olympic Village can be seen in the distance. (© **Guido Cegani; Mario De Biasi; Sergio Del Grande; Giorgio Lotti; Walter Mori; Giuseppe Pino/Mondadori Portfolio/Getty Images.**)

officers who were sportsmen or interested in sports, recruited from the ranks of the police or the border patrol and who had volunteered for this duty. From the outset, this security service already possessed a solid police training but was especially trained for the fulfillment of its special duties at the Olympic Village. The security force was intended to:

- protect the Village from trespassing by unauthorized persons and exercise a general access control function;
- settle minor disruptions of order in the Village;
- intervene in cases of criminal activity and hand over such cases to the criminal police watch stationed in the Olympic Village for further action;
- control traffic; and

- exercise a certain preventive influence by constant patrolling.

The security service was divided into small units of men and women, who served four tours of duty. Only the night-shift was armed (with pistols).

Security Precautions for the Israeli Sportsmen

Before and during the Olympic Games the various authorities received a large number of reports which announced disturbances and actions with political motives in a direct, probable or non-exclusive connection with the Olympic Games and their participants and visitors. They contained, however, scarcely any concrete clues concerning a time, place or particular object of such deeds. The responsible authorities investigated these reports. There was no specific evidence of danger to the Israeli sportsmen or equipment. Nevertheless, representatives of the police planning staff conducted a series of meetings with agents from the Israeli embassy and the Israeli Olympic team from a time beginning several months before the Olympic Games.

On August 9, 1972 an Israeli security attaché was briefed by the authorized police security authority in Munich concerning the security measures for Israeli honored guests and the Israeli Olympic team. The structure and organization of the Olympic Village and the primary responsibility of the security service in the area of the domestic right of the OC [Olympic Committee] were explained to him. The participants in this meeting were in agreement that no concrete indications of any sort concerning disturbances or assassination plots against Israeli sportsmen

> No concrete indications of any sort concerning disturbances or assassination plots against Israeli sportsmen or visitors were evident.

The 1936 "Nazi Olympics"

One reason for the lax security at the 1972 Olympics in Munich was that German officials did not want to remind visiting athletes, spectators, or officials of the last time the Olympics had taken place on German soil: 1936 in Berlin. Then, Adolf Hitler's Nazi regime was in control in Germany. The Nazis believed that the Olympics would provide a showcase for their new system, as well as for the greatness of what they believed was a superior German race. Although the International Olympic Committee, like much of the rest of the world, understood that Nazi Germany was a brutal police state, it chose to keep the games in Berlin according to a decision made in 1931, two years before Hitler took power in 1933.

Hitler was confident that German athletes would win many medals, and the German team was chosen according to Nazi racial principles, almost entirely banning Jews or others who had "inferior blood" in favor of pure Germans. This Nazi viewpoint inspired many in other countries to call for a ban of the games, although only Spain and the Soviet Union chose to not take part in the end. In the United States, although calls for a boycott were widespread and a number of Jewish athletes refused to go, others argued that Jewish or African American athletes winning medals would present a major challenge to Nazi racial ideas.

The Germans did indeed win many medals, more in fact than any other country. But the star of the 1936 Olympics was African American sprinter and long jumper Jesse Owens, who won four gold medals. Although he was outwardly cordial to Owens, Hitler was quoted behind the scenes as claiming that the athlete had a "primitive" physique that "civilized" white athletes could not hope to match, and that in future Olympics athletes of African origin should not be allowed to compete.

The 1940 Olympics were scheduled for Tokyo, Japan. But World War II, fought from 1939 to 1945, prevented any Olympics at all from taking place in either 1940 or 1944. During the war Hitler's armies conquered much of Europe, trying to extend their police state tactics and belief in racial hierarchies. They also massacred millions, mostly Jews, who they deemed unsuitable for their new racial order. Among the many sites where these killings took place was the Dachau concentration camp on the outskirts of Munich. In 1972 officials of what was then democratic West Germany remained sensitive to their country's recent past as a murderous police state and, in contrast to 1936, hoped to stage the "Happy Games."

or visitors were evident. Dissatisfaction of the Israeli security authorities with the scope of the planned security measures was not discernible.

On August 24, 1972 the final condition of the security situation in the area of public order and protection of personnel was once more discussed in conjunction with the participation of the State Office for Constitutional Protection. Although no concrete indication of any sort of threat to the Israeli Olympic team or Israeli guests was evident, a further meeting between a representative of the police command staff of Munich and a representative of the delegation of the Israeli team took place on the same day. They agreed on the security:

- of the Israeli accommodations in the Olympic Village;
- of the Israeli delegation at the youth camp;
- of the Israeli journalists;
- of the Studio 4 at the German Olympic Center during the transmission periods for Israeli television;
- of the religious services at the church center of the Olympic Village on the occasion of the Jewish New Year Festival, September 8 and 9, 1972.

Once again on August 25, 1972, an on-site-inspection in the company of a representative of the police and the security service at the Olympic Village took place at the suggestion of a representative of the Israeli delegation. On this occasion once more there were no recognizable indications of an attack against Israeli personnel or a disruption of Israeli facilities.

Security in the Munich Olympic Village Was Poor

Francie Grace

In recent years and especially after the September 11, 2001, terrorist attacks in the United States, security at major events such as the Olympics is elaborate and visible. It was different in 1972. Then, no major terrorist attacks had taken place in recent memory, and few organizers of large events saw a need for extensive security precautions. In the following viewpoint, journalist Francie Grace describes the fairly lax security at the Munich Olympic Village, making comparisons with 2001 as well as the 2004 Summer Games in Athens, Greece—where, she writes, $600 million was spent on security. Grace also quotes family members of murdered athletes who blame their loss on poor security as well as the poor response of German officials during the initial attack. The Germans, arguably, were unprepared to deal with any terrorist attack or hostage crisis.

SOURCE. Francie Grace, "Munich Massacre Remembered," *CBS News,* February 11, 2009. Copyright © 2009 by CBS News. All rights reserved. Reproduced by permission.

The Israeli athletes were enjoying a rare night out. With a break in the competition at the Munich Olympics, they went to watch a performance of [musical play] *Fiddler on the Roof* before heading back to their rooms at the Olympic Village.

Settling into bed in the early morning hours of Sept. 5, 1972, they went to sleep blissfully unaware of the eight members of a shadowy Palestinian terrorist group called Black September making their way toward the athletes' housing complex.

Dressed in track suits, their athletic bags filled with Kalashnikovs and hand grenades, the terrorists mingled among tipsy American athletes coming in for the night. With ease, they hopped the 6-foot fence surrounding the village.

Breaking in Was Easy

Shortly after 4 A.M., wrestling referee Yossef Gutfreund heard a noise at the door and went to investigate. Opening it, he saw the barrels of submachine guns.

"Take cover, boys!" he shouted before trying to close the door on the terrorists.

Startled out of their sleep, a few Israelis managed to get out a back door; others left through a window. The attackers burst into a bedroom where wrestling coach Moshe Weinberg lunged at one with a knife and was shot in the face. In another room, weightlifter Yossef Romano grabbed a gun from one terrorist and was promptly shot to death by another.

Nine other athletes—including an American competing on the Israeli team—would be captured before they could flee. They were tied hand and foot to furniture in a bloody third-floor bedroom.

Soon the world—thanks to new satellite technology that beamed the games to a billion people—would watch in horror as a drama far more compelling than any sporting event played out in the Olympic Village.

An athlete easily climbs over a locked gate in the Munich Olympic Village to leave the area immediately adjacent to where Israeli athletes are being held hostage on September 5, 1972. (© Bettmann/ Corbis.)

By the time the hostage standoff ended 21 hours later in an ill-conceived rescue attempt, 11 Israeli athletes and coaches, five terrorists and one West German police officer were dead.

The games would go on, but they'd never be the same.

Israeli commandos later hunted down and killed most of those involved in planning and carrying out the attack. And Sept. 11 [2001, in the United States] eclipsed Munich as the most shocking and outrageous terror attack the world had seen.

> 'So many fatal mistakes, such negligence, and such stupidity. . . . They should have protected my husband and the other athletes and they didn't.'

Thirty years later, there is a small monument outside the Olympic stadium honoring those who died. But time hasn't healed everything, especially for the relatives of the victims, who still battle Olympic officials and the German government over the aftermath of the killings.

"So many fatal mistakes, such negligence and such stupidity," says Ankie Spitzer, widow of fencer Andrei Spitzer. "They should have protected my husband and the other athletes and they didn't."

In an interview with CBS News Correspondent Robert Berger, Spitzer says in the wake of both the horror in Munich and the terror attacks on Sept. 11, she believes the world still has not learned its lesson.

A Widow Remembers

"I just have the feeling that the world didn't learn and doesn't know how to react to international terror," says Spitzer, wondering how it could be that Yasser Arafat [head of the Palestine Liberation Organization in 1972] could have won the Nobel peace prize, twenty years after Munich.

Israel, which had observers on the scene in Munich, has never wavered in its insistence that Arafat was behind the killings. Arafat, who is now the Palestinian President [serving from 1996 to his death in 2004], has similarly never wavered in his denial of that accusation.

Former Palestine Liberation Organization [PLO] guerrilla Mohammed Oudeh, better known by the code name Abu Daoud, wrote in a book in 1999 that Arafat was briefed on plans for the Munich hostage-taking but added that the intent was never to kill the Israeli athletes. Israeli and American intelligence experts have long implicated Oudeh and the PLO in planning the attack that ultimately left 17 dead.

By today's standards, security in Munich was almost laughable. A single chain-link fence protected the village, and athletes looking for a shortcut home often scaled it after a night out.

> There was no barbed wire, no cameras, no motion detectors, no barricades. At the entrance, unarmed guards in powder blue shirts looked more like ushers at Disneyland.

There was no barbed wire, no cameras, no motion detectors, no barricades. At the entrance, unarmed guards in powder blue shirts looked more like ushers at Disneyland.

In Athens in 2004, some $600 million will be spent on security. In Munich, only about $2 million was allocated to protect the athletes.

On that day, before the horror struck, Ankie Spitzer wasn't supposed to be in the village, but she roamed it freely with her husband nonetheless. In fact, the village was crammed with people who talked their way past the guards, entered through unattended exits or hopped the fence.

"We would walk in through the exit," she said. "They hadn't figured out they should guard that, too."

The Germans had their reasons for minimizing security. The village was less than 20 miles from the site of the Dachau [Nazi] death camp, and the hosts were determined not to give the games a militaristic look.

[Nazi ruler Adolf] Hitler's games of 1936 were still a vivid memory.

These Olympics were called "The Games of Peace and Joy," and they lived up to that nickname for 10 days, with spectacular performances by U.S. swimmer Mark Spitz and Soviet gymnast Olga Korbut.

That all changed on the morning of Sept. 5. From then on, Munich would forever be remembered for men in ski masks, smoldering helicopters and flag-draped coffins returning to Israel.

The terrorists demanded that more than 200 Palestinians be released from Israeli jails. They tossed Weinberg's bloodied body into the street to show they meant business.

A Strange Scene in the Olympic Village

Astonishingly, life went on in the village with little disruption. Rock music blared, ice cream stands did a lively business and pingpong tables were filled with players. Athletes seemed oblivious to the fact that a few hundred feet away, nine competitors were blindfolded and bound to a bedpost in Spitzer's bedroom.

As a 5 P.M. deadline to kill the hostages passed and with International Olympic Committee President Avery Brundage pressing German authorities to move the siege out of the Olympic Village, negotiators drew up a plan to fly the terrorists and their hostages to a nearby air base.

At one point, Spitzer was brought by the terrorists to a window, where they ordered him to say in German that the hostages were alive. As he got the words out, a terrorist hit him in the head with the butt of a rifle and dragged him off.

It was the last time Ankie Spitzer would see her husband alive.

At the military airport at Fürstenfeldbruck, a Boeing 707 was supposed to take the terrorists and their hostages to Cairo. Inside the plane were police dressed as crew members who were to attack the gunmen and free the victims.

Just minutes before the helicopters arrived, though, the police on the plane decided they wanted no part of a suicide mission. They took a vote and decided to get out.

"We were trained for everyday offenses, to be close to the people, unarmed—but not for an action against paramilitary-trained terrorists," former Munich police chief Manfred Schreiber said during a 1996 interview.

> '[Police] were trained for everyday offenses, to be close to the people, unarmed—but not for an action against paramilitary-trained terrorists.'

Police had to switch to a new plan. Sharpshooters were supposed to open fire as the terrorists approached the plane, killing the leaders and hoping the rest would surrender.

The Germans, though, thought there were only five terrorists when there were actually eight. And they had only five sharpshooters, whose rifles didn't have scopes or night-vision devices and who could not communicate with each other.

They weren't exactly trained snipers, either.

"I am of the opinion that I am not a sharpshooter," an officer identified as "Sniper No. 2" said in German investigative papers.

The terrorists knew they had been duped when they boarded the empty plane. They ran back toward the helicopters, and gunfire broke out.

The helicopter pilots fled, but the hostages, who were tied up inside the craft, couldn't. At one point, terrorists threw grenades in the helicopters and sprayed them with gunfire. Armored cars that would have allowed police to storm the helicopters were stuck in traffic outside the air base.

When the smoke cleared, everyone was dead except for three wounded terrorists. They would be jailed, only to be released two months later in trade for a hijacking that many people suspected was a convenient way for Germany to get rid of its problem.

In the confusion, reporters were told that all the hostages had been saved. Spitzer's father wanted to open a bottle of champagne to celebrate, but his wife refused until she saw her husband alive.

A few hours later, authorities delivered the sad news to the world.

The next day, Ankie Spitzer sat in the Olympic stadium along with the 11 Israeli Olympians who escaped. They wore white yarmulkes and maroon blazers and silently watched a hastily arranged memorial service for the dead athletes.

IOC [International Olympic Committee] President Avery Brundage never once referred to the athletes during a speech in which he praised the strength of the Olympic movement.

The Israelis, and many others who listened in shock, were outraged.

The Olympics paused only one day before resuming.

"Incredibly, they're going on with it," *Los Angeles Times* columnist Jim Murray wrote. "It's almost like having a dance at Dachau."

Since then, survivors and relatives have pushed for—but never received—a moment of silence to be held at succeeding Olympics.

Bitter Memories

"They always accused me of wanting to bring politics into the Olympics, and that the Arab countries would walk out," Ankie Spitzer said. "I said, 'Not at all. You don't even have to mention politics or Israel. Just say they were Olympians, part of the dream.'"

For 20 years, the Germans also rejected her attempts to find documents about the botched rescue, insisting there were none. An informer finally sent her some of the files 10 years ago, and others were opened for review.

Israeli secret operations forces hunted down and killed the Palestinians whom they held responsible. It was left to the relatives to seek justice from the Germans.

"Sure the terrorists were responsible, but the Germans were supposed to protect all the athletes," Ankie Spitzer said. "Afterwards, when they were taken hostage, they had no clue what to do."

At a memorial service last month [January 2009], 25 relatives returned to the Munich stadium for a one-hour ceremony at the monument to the victims—a large stone tablet placed at the bridge linking the former Olympic village to the stadium.

The names of the dead are etched in the stone in German and Hebrew, with the words: "In honor of their memory."

An Israeli flag was draped across the tablet, with 11 candles burning and fresh wreaths laid at the foot of the monument. Six Israeli flags fluttered in the wind.

Ankie Spitzer wonders whether a world shocked by Sept. 11 will learn from those who try to forget another day in September 30 years ago.

"The saddest thing for me is to see what happened in New York and get the feeling if people responded the right way 30 years ago and the world said, 'This cannot be,' that things might have been different," she said.

"My husband didn't come with a weapon; he was not a soldier. He came to participate because it was his absolute dream to be a part of it."

The German Way with Terror

Simon Reeve

In the following viewpoint, journalist and author Simon Reeve focuses on the responses of West German authorities to the terrorist attack on the Munich Olympic Village in 1972. He argues that their actions were inadequate and at times laughable. Reeve writes that documents connected to the event (unearthed in the 1990s after years of German denial) show the scale of Germany's poor response to the initial attack, as well as the negotiations that followed. According to Reeve, these new records describe the shootout at the Fürstenfeldbruck air base, where the massacre ended, as another example of bad planning and tactics. Reeve wrote the article in 2002 in the context of American preparations for a war against Iraq—a war pitched as a response to the September 11, 2001, terrorist attacks in the United States. Reeve is the author of *One Day in September: The Full Story of the 1972 Munich Olympics Massacre,* among other books.

SOURCE. Simon Reeve, "The German Way with Terror," *Spectator,* September 14, 2002. Copyright © 2002 by Spectator. All rights reserved. Reproduced by permission.

Shortly after 4 A.M. on 5 September 1972, eight heavily armed terrorists from Black September, a faction of the PLO, arrived on the outskirts of Munich and scaled a perimeter fence protecting thousands of athletes sleeping in the Olympic Village. Carrying assault rifles and grenades, they ran to Apartment One, 31 Connollystrasse, the building housing the Israeli delegation to the 1972 'Games of Peace and Joy', and crept into the foyer. Yossef Gutfreund, a 6ft 5in wrestling referee, was the only one woken by the faint sounds outside. As he crept to the door, it opened just a few inches. Sleep turned instantly to horror as the Palestinians burst inside and captured the Israelis.

Inside Apartment Three, the terrorists captured six Israeli wrestlers and weight-lifters. They hustled them into a line, and moved back towards Apartment One. Gad Tsabari, one of the wrestlers, knew the situation was desperate. With a burst of energy, he pushed a terrorist out of the way and escaped down a flight of stairs. Moshe Weinberg, his coach, tried to help him but was shot and fatally wounded.

Yossef Romano also refused to go quietly. As he was shoved upstairs to join the first group of captives, he lunged at a terrorist and was shot. Yossef, the beloved father of three young girls, fell to the floor. A second Israeli was dead.

So began the Munich Olympics massacre, the first great outrage committed in the name of Palestinian liberation outside the Middle East. The 11 September atrocities were the latest and most disastrous. Most of the blame lies with the international failure to resolve the Israeli-Palestinian crisis; but Western governments, especially the Europeans, still do not understand how to deal with terror, from Black September through to Osama bin Laden.

The Bush administration is prepared to wage war to remove Saddam from power. By contrast, European leaders were lukewarm about tackling the Taleban in Afghanistan, and remain reluctant to tackle Iraq. The German leader, Gerhard Schroder is even campaigning for re-election on the slogan that a vote for him is a vote against war.

For many Americans, the 30th anniversary of Munich is a timely reminder of German and European impotence in the face of terrorism. The German authorities were criminally negligent during the Munich crisis. Policemen ludicrously disguised as chefs left food outside No. 31, thinking they could somehow overpower the well-armed militants. Officials literally begged the Palestinians to give up and offered them cash to surrender. They could not believe that the Palestinians were mining the most expensive Games ever held, mounted partly in an attempt to expunge memories of the Holocaust.

> The German authorities were criminally negligent during the Munich crisis.

Around the globe news of the attack was leading broadcasts as the Palestinians issued their demands: they wanted to swap their remaining nine hostages for 234 prisoners held in Israeli jails and two from German prisons. It was a straight, if unequal, exchange of souls, and the first deadline was 9 A.M.

The Germans told Luttif Issa, the Black September leader, that Israeli officials needed longer to locate the prisoners, and the first deadline was extended. By 10 A.M. panic was spreading through the German government at the realisation that neither side was prepared to compromise.

Olympic organisers soon suspended the Games and more than 50,000 spectators began congregating around the perimeter fence. A television audience of 900 million viewers in more than 100 countries watched as the archetypal figure of a terrorist, a stocking on his head, emerged from No. 31 to check the position of police officers. Broadcasters cleared their schedules as the siege became global theatre.

Eventually the Germans attempted a half-hearted rescue operation. Twelve poorly trained police officers climbed on to the roof above No. 31 Connollystrasse in preparation for an assault. Thousands of spectators, watching the police from a hillock just outside the perimeter fence, yelled tactical advice as at a pantomime ('Get down! Get down!'). Eventually the officers realised that the terrorists were watching events unfolding live on their own televisions.

By early evening Issa was demanding a plane and told officials that the hostages and terrorists would be flying to the Middle East. Some German officials were delighted that they could move the crisis away from the Olympics, while others decided to launch a rescue as the hostages boarded the plane. They agreed to shuttle the terrorists and hostages in two helicopters to Fürstenfeldbruck airfield outside Munich, where a Boeing 727 would fly them out of the country.

Just after 10 P.M. a bus took the Palestinians and blindfolded Israelis to helicopters waiting in the Olympic plaza. Hans Dietrich Genscher, the German interior minister, was watching. "One, two, three, four . . ." he said, gasping as he counted eight terrorists. All day the Germans had thought there were only five Palestinians, and there were only five snipers waiting at Fürstenfeldbruck.

Worse followed. The Germans had 17 officers hidden on the 727 to capture or kill the first two terrorists, but they grew worried about their mission, and fearful for their own safety in the plane. An officer held a ballot and, in an act of sheer cowardice, all 17 men voted to leave. The helicopters carrying the terrorists were already landing and there was no time to hide a new squad on the 727.

The Palestinians clambered on to the tarmac, found the plane empty and realised it was a trap. The snipers opened up with two inaccurate shots and the 'rescue' began. There was instant chaos. The terrorists ducked into shadows under the choppers and began sweeping the airport with bullets.

The battle went on for over an hour. German officers sheltered in airport buildings, and it certainly seems possible that their bravery was discouraged by latent anti-Semitism. Eventually armoured cars blundered on to the airfield. The gunner in one car shot two men on his own side and the terrorists thought they were about to be machine-gunned. In one helicopter a terrorist shot four of the hostages before another man leapt out on to the tarmac and tossed a grenade inside. The explosion ignited the fuel tank, and the captive Israelis burned. Another terrorist then shot the Israelis in the other helicopter. Germans present at the airfield are

The remains of one of the helicopters used by the terrorists to flee the Olympic Village sit on the tarmac of the Munich airport. It was destroyed the night of September 5, 1972, by a hand grenade explosion and fire. Several of the bound hostages were killed inside. (© **Rolls Press/ Popperfoto/Getty Images.**)

still haunted by their screams. All 11 Israelis were killed. Three Palestinians survived.

> For more than two decades German officials refused to give information about what happened at Munich, fearing accusations of anti-Semitism.

For more than two decades German officials refused to give information about what really happened at Munich, fearing accusations of anti-Semitism, and claiming there was only one short report on the attack. But a few years ago a whistleblower revealed a hoard of thousands of files. The errors made by German officials are staggering. There were only five poorly trained snipers, with no walkie-talkies, inadequate rifles, poor lighting, no flak-jackets or helmets, and no proper rifle sights or infrared equipment. Interpol had issued an alert just weeks before the Games that Palestinian militants were grouping in Europe, and German intelligence warned the Munich police of Palestinian plans to do 'something'. And yet nothing was done to protect the most vulnerable guests. The cover-up continues: German officials have recently tried to silence witnesses, and film footage showing events at Fürstenfeldbruck has been stolen.

Thirty years after the massacre the tragedy continues to echo around the Middle East. Some European politicians still do not seem to understand that stopping similar terrorist attacks requires governments to pursue a twin-track approach: resolving the crisis in the Middle East to the benefit of both sides, and aggressively targeting the psychopaths who lead the terror organisations.

Sartre on Munich 1972

Elizabeth Bowman

In the following viewpoint, scholar Elizabeth Bowman provides a translation and introductory summary of an article written by French philosopher Jean-Paul Sartre in 1972. Sympathetic to the Palestinian cause, Sartre's article was first published in the short-lived left-wing French periodical *La Cause du peuple,* or *The People's Cause*. Sartre himself was one of the most prominent philosophers of the second half of the twentieth century.

According to Bowman's translation, Sartre's viewpoint is that terrorism is the only weapon available to Palestinians in their "war" against Israel. Sartre also criticizes those who condemn Palestinian terrorism while applauding similar methods used by Israel, Arab governments, or even the French in their fight against Algerian independence in the 1950s and 1960s. He goes on to lay the blame for the Munich massacre on West German police rather than Palestinian terrorists who, thanks to the event, brought the world's attention to problems of the time. Bowman is the author of numerous academic articles on Sartre's thinking.

The first internationally staged "terrorist" event—the Palestinian kidnapping of Israeli athletes—occurred in Munich, Germany, during the 1972 Summer Olympics. Sartre's article "About Munich" concerns this event.

This summary of events is based on reports in the *New York Times* of Sept. 6, 7, and 9, 1972. At roughly 5 A.M. local time on [Sept. 5], 1972, five Palestinians joined three others near the living quarters of the Israeli athletes and attacked. Two athletes were immediately killed; many fled; nine were held hostage (three were coaches, four were athletes, and two were Israeli security men). By 9 A.M. the kidnappers had identified themselves as the Palestinian Black September group and negotiations began with the Munich police chief, Dr. Manfred Schreiber; the Interior Minister, Hans Dietrich Genscher; the Bavarian state Interior Minister, Bruno Merk; the President of the International Olympic Committee, Avery Brundage; the Arab League's representative in Bonn, Mohammed Khatib; the Tunisian Ambassador; and others. The Palestinians demanded the release of 200 Palestinian prisoners in Israel and safe passage out of West Germany. Golda Meir, then the Israeli Prime Minister, refused any concessions.

The negotiators and Palestinians agreed to fly the Israelis and the Palestinians by helicopter to a near-by military base where they would board a plane for Tunisia. Around 9 P.M., three helicopters arrived in the Olympic Village. The eight Palestinians, nine Israelis, and three German officials boarded the helicopters and flew to the nearby military base. Mr. Brundage gave the instruction that the Palestinians were not to leave the country with the Israelis. As the transfer from the helicopters to the airplane was being initiated around 10:30PM, shots were fired. Within minutes, all the Israeli athletes and five Palestinians were killed; three Palestinians were wounded and later arrested.

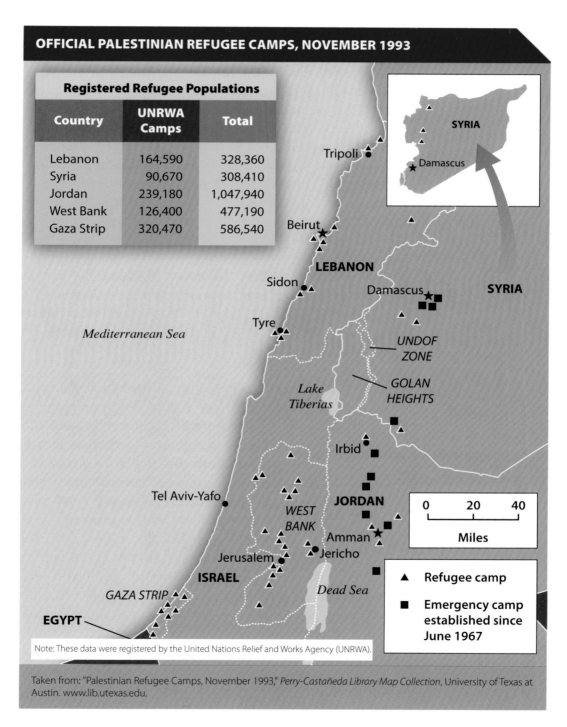

OFFICIAL PALESTINIAN REFUGEE CAMPS, NOVEMBER 1993

Registered Refugee Populations

Country	UNRWA Camps	Total
Lebanon	164,590	328,360
Syria	90,670	308,410
Jordan	239,180	1,047,940
West Bank	126,400	477,190
Gaza Strip	320,470	586,540

SYRIA
Damascus

Tripoli

Beirut

LEBANON

Sidon

Damascus   SYRIA

Tyre

Mediterranean Sea

UNDOF ZONE

GOLAN HEIGHTS

Lake Tiberias

Irbid

Tel Aviv-Yafo

WEST BANK   JORDAN

Amman

Jerusalem   Jericho

ISRAEL

GAZA STRIP   Dead Sea

EGYPT

0   20   40

Miles

▲ Refugee camp

■ Emergency camp established since June 1967

Note: These data were registered by the United Nations Relief and Works Agency (UNRWA).

Taken from: "Palestinian Refugee Camps, November 1993," *Perry-Castañeda Library Map Collection*, University of Texas at Austin. www.lib.utexas.edu.

The *New York Times* of Sept. 7, 1972, quoted the Munich police chief Dr. Schreiber: "I had the feeling we gave the first shots." And the Bavarian state Interior Minister Bruno Merk was quoted as saying: "The firing was started by the police, naturally."

On Sept. 9, 1972, the *New York Times* reported that the U.S. government had announced "the formation of an intelligence committee to deter international political terrorism in cooperation with intelligence services of friendly foreign countries." The committee would be made up of senior officials of the State Dept., the CIA, the FBI, and the DIA.

Jean-Paul Sartre, "About Munich"

Translated by Elizabeth Bowman: *La Cause du peuple— J'accuse,* No. 29, du 15 Oct. 1972. (Republished in *Les Nouvelles litteraires,* 11–17 Nov., 1982, under the title "A New Sartre Scandal.")

Those who affirm the sovereignty of the Israeli state and also believe Palestinians have a right to sovereignty for the same reason, and who take the Palestinian question as fundamental, must admit that the Israeli establishment's policy is literally crazy and deliberately aims at avoiding all possible solutions to this problem. It is therefore politically accurate to say that a state of war exists between Israel and the Palestinians. In this war the Palestinians' only weapon is terrorism. It is a terrible weapon but the oppressed poor have no other, and the French who approved FLN terrorism against the French must approve in turn the Palestinians' terrorist action. This abandoned, betrayed, exiled people can show its courage and the force of its hate only by organizing deadly attacks. Of course these should be viewed politi-

> [Terrorism] is a terrible weapon but the oppressed poor have no other.

cally, by assessing the intended results against those actually obtained. We would also need to settle the highly ambiguous question of the real relationships among Arab governments, none of which is socialist nor has socialist tendencies, and the feddayin, which leads us to ask whether the Palestinians' primary enemies may not be these feudal dictatorships, several of which have supported them verbally while at the same time trying to massacre them, and whether the first effort of the Palestinians, whose war necessarily dedicates them to socialism, must not be to side with the peoples of the Middle East against those Arab states which oppress them. But these problems cannot be treated in an article.

It must be said that for those who agree with the terrorist attacks to which the Israeli establishment and the Arab dictatorships have reduced the Palestinians, it

A Black September fighter emerges on the balcony of the Olympic Village building where Israeli hostages are being held. (© **The Sydney Morning Herald/ Fairfax Media/Getty Images.**)

seems perfectly outrageous that the French press and a segment of opinion should judge the Munich attack an intolerable outrage while one has often read dry reports without comment of strikes in Tel Aviv that cost several human lives. The principle of terrorism is that one must kill. And even if one is resigned to that, it remains, as it was for Albert Memmi who agreed with the Algerians' struggle, inexcusable after an explosion to see mutilated bodies or a child's severed head. But if one can admit it, then we must in fact recognize that the Munich attack succeeded perfectly. It took place amidst an international sporting event that attracted hundreds of journalists from all countries; for this reason it assumed world importance, and, thereby, put the Palestinian question before the whole world more tragically than at the UN where the Palestinians are not represented. The Palestinians aimed not at massacring the hostages on the spot but at taking them to an Arab country where they would have negotiated an exchange of Palestinian prisoners in Israel for the hostages. Similarly, while we disagree with the Israeli government on all other points, we can understand that, being at war with the Palestinians, Israel would reject all concessions. Regardless of how one judges such intransigence, it too was on display before international opinion.

> The attack at the Olympics historically unveiled, for all to see, the despair of the Palestinian combatants and the horrible courage this despair gives them.

The only guilty party was the Munich police. For we now know that the Palestinians did not explode the device that was to take them out, but instead everyone, feddayin and hostages, was killed by police bullets. That there had been disagreements between Munich and Bonn does not excuse the cops. Quite the contrary.

Thus the attack at the Olympics historically unveiled, for all to see, the despair of the Palestinian combatants and the horrible courage this despair gives them. While tactically it did not advance their cause, it showed and established better than any speech at the UN both that we must now, right away, solve the Palestinian problem and that this problem has become everyone's. The violent indignation shown by "noble" hearts in the press concerns neither Palestinians nor Israelis. These good apostles would have Israelis killed in Israel rather than disrupt the noble and classical order of the Olympic games, this sacred ceremony from ancient Greece. This reaction was foreseeable and will soon give way to a more realistic view. It is meanwhile no less ignoble.

It Was the Costliest Day in Olympic History

Jim Murray

The following viewpoint was written by Jim Murray, a sportswriter for the Los Angeles Times who was in Munich to cover the games at the time of the attack. Written before the climax of the massacre at Fürstenfeldbruck airfield, Murray's article describes the scene in the Olympic Village earlier that day, September 5, 1972, when few athletes understood the true extent of the attack and observers largely went about their ordinary business. The viewpoint also shows the author's shock and surprise at the two killings that had already taken place and completely changed the nature of the event. Murray, who died in 1998, won a Pulitzer Prize in 1990 and was a fourteen-time winner of the National Sportscasters and Sportswriters Association award for Sportswriter of the Year.

I stood on a rooftop balcony on the Connollystrasse in the Olympic village Tuesday and witnessed an Olympic event Baron de Coubertin never dreamed of and the purpose of which is as arcane to me as the discus, the team foil, the hammer, individual epee, or Greco-Roman wrestling.

An Arab rifle team, arriving late, scorned the small bore rifle, three positions, the free pistol (silhouette) and introduced a new event to the Olympic program—murder.

Dead were Moshe Weinberg, Yossi Romano, both 33, and, maybe, the Olympic Games, age 30 centuries.

There was great concern the Olympic Games were getting too costly and they are. When they start costing lives, there's a new name for them—and it's not "games."

> "Eight guys with hate in their hearts and guns in their hands have turned this whole billion-mark festival into a Middle East incident."

They became a forum for political protest in 1968 and now they've become a forum for political assassination. Maybe they'll bomb the next one.

Eight guys with hate in their hearts and guns in their hands have turned this whole billion-mark festival into a Middle East incident. They have hijacked the Olympics.

I arrived at the village at 9:30. Most of the non-German-speaking people still had no inkling that the Olympic Games were in the hands of an unofficial, non-sanctioned committee.

The Germans, who had not halted eight armed, homicidal uncredentialed terrorists, now proceeded to solve the problem by barring journalists armed with dangerous pencils.

But the Germans are undone by their own thoroughness in this Olympics. Obviously under instructions not to betray any officiousness reminiscent of you-know-who and his brown-shirted you-know-whats, they have dressed their cops in powder blue suits with white caps as if they were on their way to punting in the park with their picnic baskets. Underneath the pansy costumes were guys who were just as tough and muscular as the

The Revival of the Olympic Games

The origin of the Olympic Games goes back to ancient Greece, when various independent city-states began competing with one another in athletic events as early as 776 B.C. Held every four years near the town of Olympia, these ancient games were acknowledged as a period of peace, when war would be suspended so that athletes and others could travel in safety.

The modern Olympic tradition began in 1896. Although proud modern Greeks had held competitions on a smaller scale for several decades, French nobleman Baron Pierre de Coubertin believed the event could be a truly international one, and he started the International Olympic Committee (IOC) in 1894. Coubertin believed in the nobility of struggle and competition, and also that the event could promote peace among nations. Following his lead, the IOC agreed to hold the 1896 Olympics in Athens, the capital of Greece. Most events were track and field events, some of which, such as short sprints or the throwing of the discus, had been contested at the ancient games. One new event was the marathon race, eventually fixed at 26.2 miles. The event was organized to commemorate the legendary run of an ancient Athenian messenger who took the news of a military victory over invad-ers some twenty miles to Athens before dying of exhaustion.

Only fourteen nations attended the 1896 Olympics, and the event struggled over the next years. But beginning with the 1908 games in London, more and more nations began to take part in an increasing number of competitions, and the Olympics grew to be the world's dominant sporting event. In 1924, the first Winter Olympics was held in Chamonix, France, as a counterpart to the Summer Games. Until 1992, the winter and summer games were held in the same year, but then the schedule was changed to hold one or the other event every two years.

Another major shift in recent years was the decision to allow professional, or paid, athletes to take part. Baron de Coubertin believed that only amateurs should be eligible, but, after intensive lobbying, the competition was opened to all athletes, including professional ones, in 1988. Meanwhile, women athletes have taken part in the games since 1900, a strong contrast to ancient Greece when women were not allowed to compete at all. Women were, however, restricted to certain events; only in 1984 in Los Angeles, for instance, did women first compete in the marathon.

Athletes at the 1972 Games play chess on a giant set in the Munich Olympic Village. (© **Rich Clarkson/Time Life Pictures/Getty Images**.)

rubber truncheon crowd of 1936, but the impossibility of 250 guards sealing off 10,000 people is apparent. The Germans, as usual, had trouble with their occupation.

Inside the Olympic village, the athletes treated the whole event as just another heat in the high jump. Bicyclists bicycled. Runners ran intervals. Occasionally, a crowd would wander out to the checkpoint on the Connollystrasse or the main forecourt of the Olympic village, where now were parked armored cars, tanks, fire wagons, and what seemed like 2,000 guys with walkie-talkies. The chief of police of Munich was in his command post in an olive green van crackling with telephones.

But the American sprinters played hard rock music and played cards noisily by the main gate, the milk bars did a lively business, shotputters compared pushes and a huge crowd filled the television center to cheer lustily as the Cuban, Teofilo Stevenson, beat the American, Duane Bobick.

To most, the affair in Building 31 seemed like a minor affair, like a divot in the long jump runway. It was something that can't be decided with a pole, a shoe, a spear, a paddle or a cross-bar, so how the hell important can it be? If they make it a sanctioned quadrennial event, the athletes and coaches might explore it. But the rank-and-file track-and-field man has never had much interest in nonwinning times in the pistol shoot.

The decathloner, Bruce Jenner, busy getting a rubdown for an event that may not now take place, looked in annoyance at the Arab lookout silhouetted on his balcony vigil and said, "It's all a bunch of. . . .Why do we have to cancel a day?

"We can walk around that building on the way to the track, can't we? We don't have to go through it."

The point is, the Olympics may find the event in Building 31 one they can't walk around. Now that there is blood on the Olympic symbol and terrorism drew crowds to the Olympic Park the 1,500-meter heats couldn't dream of, they may have to award iron crosses instead of gold medals.

And the Olympic motto may have a fourth to go along with "citius," "altius," "fortius." It will now be "higher, faster, stronger." And "slaughter."

Sports Can Seem Inconsequential in Moments of Crisis, but They Reflect Our Humanity

Philip Hersh

After the full extent of the Munich massacre became known, Olympic events for the next day, September 6, 1972, were cancelled for a memorial ceremony. At the memorial, the International Olympic Committee's president, Avery Brundage, made the announcement that the games would continue to their completion. In the following viewpoint (written just after the September 11, 2001, terrorist attacks in the United States), journalist Philip Hersh describes how Brundage and other officials reached that decision. He also notes that, although many Olympic athletes were surprised at the choice, most decided to stay and take part in their competitions, often with a heavy heart.

Frank Shorter was standing on an Olympic Village balcony with several U.S. track teammates, including Kenny Moore, when the impact of what was happening nearby became clear.

It was the morning of Tuesday, Sept. 5, 1972, the 10th day of the Munich Olympic Games. Across the Olympic Village, in the building at 31 Connollystrasse, terrorists from the Black September faction of the Palestine Liberation Organization had taken Israeli hostages.

The U.S. athletes could see armored personnel carriers being moved into a staging area. They soon learned some of the Israelis had been killed.

"Our first reaction was people died, and nothing else could be so important as that, so there is no reason for the Olympics to continue, and we just have to go home," Shorter recalled from his home in Boulder, Colo.

Five days later, after the hostage crisis had ended with the deaths of 11 members of Israel's Olympic delegation, Shorter became the first U.S. runner since 1908 to win the Olympic marathon. Moore was fourth. Both think it was important that they stayed and that the 1972 Olympics did not end with the tragedy for which they always will be remembered.

"I supported the decision to continue the Games then, and I support it more firmly now," Moore said. "For the sake of the athletes and the [Olympic] ideal, you have

> 'A great moral advance in our world came 2,500 years ago, when the Greeks put down their arms and felt the sacredness of competition rather than conquest.'

to go on. Sport brings us together and is an antidote to hate. It is about all we've got in the long term.

"A great moral advance in our world came 2,500 years ago, when the Greeks put down their arms and felt the sacredness of competition rather than conquest, that there was more honor in outrunning a man than killing him."

For the decisions about when sport should go on in the wake of Tuesday's terrorist attacks, a tragedy of far larger statistical proportions than the Munich massacre, public sentiment and the athletes' feelings have been given serious consideration.

The decisions about the fate of the 1972 Olympics were nearly all made by one man, Avery Brundage. He was then the 84-year-old, lame-duck president of the International Olympic Committee.

Brundage, a graduate of the University of Illinois and a Chicago resident who died in 1975, had been the U.S. Olympic Committee president who disdainfully rejected pleas to have the U.S. boycott the 1936 Nazi Olympics in Berlin. Three months before the Berlin Games began, Brundage said, "The anti-Nazi outcry in this country is the work of alien agitators, Communists and certain Jews."

Thundered Brundage during a Sept. 6, 1972, memorial service at the Munich Olympic Stadium: "The Games must go on!"

The decision of whether an athlete should stay at what was to have been a German Olympics of reconciliation remained, in theory, with each individual.

Jos Hermens of the Netherlands, a 22-year-old distance runner in 1972 and now one of world's leading track and field agents, was among the few athletes who left. Ten Norwegian team handball players left but were forced to return when the international handball federation threatened to hold Norway's national federation financially responsible for gate receipts lost in canceled games.

Athletic Achievement at the Munich Games

Although the 1972 Munich Olympics was dominated by the killings of Israeli athletes in a terrorist attack, there were indeed memorable athletic feats as well. One great performer was American swimmer Mark Spitz, who won seven gold medals, more than any athlete had ever won at a single Olympics and a record not broken until 2008. Spitz also set new world records in each of those seven events. A Jew, Spitz left the Games before the closing ceremony for fear of another terrorist attack. Meanwhile another swimmer, Australian Shane Gould, took three gold medals at the age of fifteen.

Another great performance came from Soviet gymnast Olga Korbut. Korbut won a total of three gold medals (one in a team competition), but she also became a media star, being an appealing personality from a nation then very slowly opening itself up to the outside world. She was eventually featured on the cover of *Time* magazine in a photograph subtitled, "She's Perfect," reflecting a perfect "ten" she had received from judges.

In running events a Finn, Lasse Viren, took gold in the 5,000 and 10,000 meter races. Among those he beat was American Steve Prefontaine, a hopeful who died in a 1975 car accident and who was one of the leaders in the effort to gain further financial support for the training of Olympic athletes. Meanwhile Frank Shorter, a friend of Prefontaine's, was the first American to win a gold medal in the marathon since 1908.

The US basketball team, which at that time was still made up entirely of nonprofessional players, had won gold in every Olympic competition held from 1936 to 1968. But it did not win in Munich. In one of the great controversies of the event, the US team lost to the Soviets in the basketball final, 51–50, after confusion over a timeout. Team members continue to reject their silver medals due to the controversy.

"They were calling those Olympics the 'Happy Games,'" Hermens said Friday. "If you give a party and someone gets killed, you don't go on.

"I went to the memorial service, where I was expecting them to say the Games would be stopped. When Brundage said they would go on, I was shocked. I left immediately. No one tried to convince me to stay."

Hermens left four days before the 5,000-meter race in which he had hoped to be a finalist. The Games went on.

They had continued during the first 12 hours of the hostage crisis, which ended early in the morning of Sept. 6 after a botched rescue attempt at a Munich airfield. The Olympics were suspended 24 hours, from midafternoon Sept. 5 until midafternoon the next day, before continuing to their conclusion.

Willye White, who grew up in the Mississippi delta at the time of "lynchings, cross burnings and the Ku Klux Klan," was competing in the last of her five Olympics at the Munich Games. She will not forgive Brundage for letting the Games continue.

"I grew up in terror," White said. "If you haven't walked that road, you don't understand how I felt in Munich.

"He [Brundage] was an ugly, unkind man. He ruined more lives for Olympians than anyone else. All the derogatory things involving the United States and the Olympics began with him."

Marc Hodler, 82, of Switzerland, who recently has come to be known as the conscience of the IOC for his whistle-blowing in the corruption scandal, is one of a half-dozen current IOC members who also were members at the time of the Munich Games. Hodler is not sure the decision to continue was right.

"German authorities were very confident the kidnapping could be stopped peacefully," he said Thursday from his home in Bern. "We made the decision to continue [before] the attack at the airport. It became a very doubtful decision later. This was not possible to foresee. The situation was very complex."

It was a situation Brundage tried to manage by himself. He did it with the autocratic style that had marked his two decades as IOC president and with the anachronistic view that saw the Olympics as a gathering of pure amateurs.

In criticizing Brundage's decision to continue, *New York Times* columnist Red Smith cited a bitter joke making the rounds in Munich: "These are professional killers. Avery doesn't recognize them."

Brundage, whose presidency ended with the Closing Ceremonies in Munich, did not recognize that the incoming president, Lord Killanin of Ireland, should have a role in the decision-making. Killanin, attending the Olympic sailing competition on Germany's north coast when the hostage crisis began, later decried Brundage's actions.

In his book, *My Olympic Years*, Killanin recounted how Brundage had told him not to return to Munich to help deal with the crisis, a suggestion Killanin disregarded.

"[IOC member Count de Beaumont] and I were particularly upset by Brundage's seemingly insane attempt to deal with the whole situation himself," wrote Killanin, who died in 1999.

At 3:51 P.M Sept. 5, Brundage announced the Games would be suspended 24 hours starting at 4 P.M., but some events went on a few hours after that. He also called a memorial service for Sept. 6 at 10 A.M. for the one Israeli then known to be dead, wrestling coach Moshe Weinberg.

Brundage's prominent role in meetings of the German government crisis team also rankled Killanin and other IOC members. They thought, as Killanin wrote, this was a "crisis far beyond the scope of the IOC."

It was only at Killanin's urging that an IOC emergency executive board meeting was called for 7 P.M. Sept. 5.

With Brundage absent from the meeting, the executive board endorsed his plan and called a meeting of the IOC's 75 members for 10 P.M. Sept. 5. Voting before they knew what would happen at the airport, the IOC members unanimously backed Brundage.

The Olympic flag is flown at half mast during a special memorial for the killed Israeli athletes at Munich's Olympic Stadium on September 6, 1972. (© Jerry Cooke/ **Sports Illustrated/Getty Images.**)

James Worrall, 87, of Canada, was an IOC member at the time. Asked what would have been lost had the Games been stopped, Worrall had no easy response.

"That is a good question that raises moral issues we perhaps didn't deal with adequately at the time," Worrall said. "There was a feeling the Olympic Games were important and shouldn't be stopped.

"I think we made the right decision at the time, and I haven't changed my mind after all the years. God knows, though, if it happened again, I might feel differently."

Prince Alexandre de Merode of Belgium, 67, another current member who also was on the IOC in 1972, thought the body should "take the same decision again if this happens again."

Worrall and several other IOC members did turn on Brundage after the IOC leader used the memorial service to criticize African nations that had threatened to boycott the Munich Games over the presence of Rhodesia.

> 'We went through shock and grief, and as we walked back from the memorial service we began to realize the Games had to go on or the terrorists would have won.'

"Brundage drew a parallel between an unprecedented, savage, murderous attack on human beings and an attack on the universality of the Olympic movement," Worrall said. "That did not go over well with any of us."

Nearly all the athletes went back to being athletes. White, a longtime youth services worker in Chicago, had finished 11th in the long jump Aug. 31.

"You're there, so what are you going to do?" she said. "You compete."

Shorter said: "We went through shock and grief, and as we walked back from the memorial service we began to realize the Games had to go on or the terrorists would have won.

"The athletes realized the only thing we could do affirmatively was to compete. That isn't callous and has nothing to do with personal aggrandizement. It is a primordial emotion that has to do with the survival instinct."

Hermens can understand why most athletes made that choice, and is "not judging them" because he acted differently.

"Sport is nice, but you have to draw the line some-where," Hermens said, "whether it is two killings, 13 or 5,000. For me, the line was clear."

For Moore a different line became equally clear, the one separating innocence from reality.

"All the illusions that we had some kind of perfect, inviolable sanctuary in the Olympic Village ended when the murderers charged in," he said. "It showed how the world could be."

That it only has grown worse is what dismays Her-mens most.

"The basis of the things that happened in Munich are still happening," he said. "Thirty years later, we have not learned the lesson."

German Authorities Helped Surviving Palestinian Attackers Escape

Jason Burke

Of the eight Palestinian terrorists who launched the Munich Olympic attack, five were killed during the airport shootout the evening of September 5, 1972. The other three were taken prisoner by West German police. In the following viewpoint, British author Jason Burke touches on a feature of the Munich massacre that remains controversial: the release of the three terrorists in October that year. Burke writes that the three survivors were possibly released as the result of a suspicious airplane hijacking. On October 29 a passenger jet owned by Lufthansa (a German airline company and national flagship carrier) was hijacked in Lebanon, and its alleged hijackers demanded the release of the three Munich terrorists. The West German government agreed to the

---

demand, and the three were flown to Libya where they received an enthusiastic welcome. The viewpoint notes that, although German authorities have never admitted to staging a false hijacking, many sources have acknowledged this claim. According to Burke the Germans hoped that, by letting the Munich attackers go, they could prevent further terrorist attacks in their country. Burke is the author of *Al-Qaeda: The True Story of Radical Islam* and *On the Road to Kandahar: Travels Through Conflict in the Islamic World*.

Black September, the Palestinian terror group that killed 11 Israeli athletes at the 1972 Munich Olympics, was allowed by the German government to hijack a passenger jet two months later to provide a "cover story" for the release of the three gunmen captured at the scene.

According to *One Day in September*—an Oscar-nominated documentary which is to be released in Britain in May [2000]—Bonn [West Germany] indicated to the terrorist group that it would give in to their demands should a certain aircraft—carrying no women and children—be hijacked. The Germans were keen to release the three jailed terrorists to avoid Black September fulfilling threats to carry out a series of bombings and hijackings.

On 29 October, 1972—not even eight weeks after the Munich attack—a Lufthansa Boeing 727 on its way from Damascus, Syria, to Frankfurt was hijacked by two terrorists as it left Beirut airport. There were only 11 passengers on board, all male. The pilot was told to fly to Munich and the terrorists' demands were relayed to Bonn. Within hours the German Chancellor, Willy Brandt, gave in and the three men were handed over. The Israelis were not consulted.

All three Black September men had been arrested during a botched attempt by German authorities to rescue the Israeli athletes taken hostage in the Olympic Village. Nine hostages and five terrorists died in the

In an event that many sources acknowledge was staged, German police vehicles and officers surround a plane during the hostage exchange at the Munich airport in October 1972.
(© Rolls Press/ Popperfoto/Getty Images.)

shoot-out. Two of the surviving terrorists were later killed by Mossad—the Israeli secret service—but Jamal Al-Gashey, the third, has survived in hiding. He gave his first, and only, interview to the *One Day in September* team. "An agreement had been made with the German government for our release after the hijacking of a Lufthansa plane," Al-Gashey told researchers. "I found out later."

Palestinian and German Sources

Though Brandt himself denied any deal, Al-Gashey's allegations are supported by a range of senior German, Palestinian and Israeli intelligence and political sources. Ulrich Wegener, then a key aide of the Interior Minister and the founder of GSG-9, the Germans' crack counter-terrorist unit, said Bonn did not want to risk confronting the Palestinians after the attack on the Olympics.

Earlier in the year Lufthansa had allegedly paid a ransom of $5 million (£3.2m) after the hijack of a jet flying to Yemen. "At this time the German government thought they could negotiate with terrorists, and [that] they could give them money [or] something else to get rid of them," Wegener said.

> The German government thought they could negotiate with terrorists, and [that] they could give them money [or] something else to get rid of them."

The return of the hostages was celebrated in the Middle East. But the Israelis were stunned. Golda Meir, the Prime Minister, decided that their release—and the conciliatory attitude of Bonn—had to be answered. Within hours of hearing the news that Al-Gashey and his comrades were free, she authorised Mossad to launch "Operation Wrath of God." For the next 20 years, Israeli agents tracked down those connected with the Munich attack and killed them.

Many relatives are bitter about Bonn's acts. "Of course I blame the terrorists," Ankie Spitzer, widow of the Israeli fencing coach who died, said. "But most of all I blame the German authorities."

The Munich Attack Inaugurated the Modern Era of Terrorism

Erich Follath and Gerhard Spörl

The Munich massacre garnered renewed attention in 2005 when Hollywood director Steven Spielberg released *Munich,* a major film that depicts the attack and focuses on a fictionalized version of Israel's retribution against the attackers. In the following viewpoint, German journalists Erich Follath and Gerhard Spörl use the occasion of the film's release to contrast Israel's response to the Munich massacre with America's response to the September 11, 2001, terrorist attacks. At the heart of their arguments are suggestions that, when responding to terrorism, governments should take into account national values and ideals. The authors also state that Munich established a continuing pattern of behavior on the part of both attackers and the attacked.

These are cheerful games, almost un-Germanically cheerful, say foreign visitors, half surprised and half sarcastic, and that's exactly how the Germans have planned, prepared and staged the 1972 Munich Olympic Games. The country is presenting its best side to the world, and even the major conflicts raging out there in the real world seem half-forgotten under the clear blue skies of these late summer days. How beautiful, how hopeful, how deceptive.

September 5 began a few hours ago. The night air is mild and sensuous as a few young, slightly tipsy American athletes return home after a night on the town. They have to climb a fence to reach their quarters in the Olympic Village. They think nothing of it when they run into eight other young men, who seem to be about to do the same thing.

"Too bad the bars and beer gardens close up so early here," says one of the inebriated Americans. "Otherwise we could grab a beer together." The remark seems to make no impact whatsoever on the eight strangers. What's wrong with them, the Americans wonder, are they just unfriendly, or what? "Oh well," offers another of the tipsy Americans into the strange silence, "but I do think they need some help." The men are all young, they want some excitement and there is no one there to stand in their way—not a policeman in sight, and there are no German Shepherds in the Olympic Village. The two groups help each other scale the two-meter (6.5 foot) barrier, walk a few steps together and part ways. "Good night and have fun," the Americans call out.

"Germany's Worst Night"

The eight silent men are not Olympic athletes—they're Palestinians and fun is about the last thing they're looking for. They've burned their passports and made the kinds of arrangements one would make when expecting to die. They pull stocking masks from their duffle bags and load their automatic pistols with ammunition. At 4:35 A.M., an hour before sunrise, they storm the apartments housing the Israeli athletes. Their goal is to take as many hostages as possible, Jewish hostages. They are prepared to kill them, if necessary. Their goal is to send a message to the world, a signal.

That was how "West Germany's worst night" began, as German newspaper Die Zeit described it, and how Munich's cheerful games were suddenly transformed into tragic games. By the time the nightmare ended 21 hours later at the Fürstenfeldbruck airport, the eight Palestinian terrorists had murdered 11 Israeli hostages and one German police officer. The images were gruesome: the dead athletes lying, bound tightly together, in destroyed helicopters. The unbelievably amateurish attempt to save the hostages was a miserable failure. Then Chancellor Willy Brandt summarized the incident with the devastating conclusion that Munich was "shocking testimony to German helplessness."

> The unbelievably amateurish attempt to save the hostages was a miserable failure.

But Munich is more than that. It's the birthplace of terrorism in the postwar world, a world that doesn't know what's in store for it, a shocked world that is rendered speechless, just as it was 29 years later on another day under a [Impressionist painter Henri] Matisse-blue sky, September 11, 2001. . . .

The Birth of Modern Terrorism

The Germans, who had actually planned to show the world their democratic face at these Olympic Games, were accused of incompetence and helplessness, especially by the Israelis. Although the games continued after a day of mourning, the 1972 Munich Olympics would go down in history as a preview of a new, monstrous dimension of terror.

For the Israelis, but also for others, Munich fits into a sort of German triad: Munich, the city of [Nazi leader Adolf] Hitler; Munich, the city that symbolized the West's policy of appeasement, when it kowtowed to the German leader in 1938 in an effort to avert war; and now there was Munich, city of shame, where Jews were taken hostage and murdered, simply because they were Jews.

This is multilayered and ambiguous material, even for a pro like [film director Steven] Spielberg, who probably knew early on that he could be giving up his reputation as a universally admired wunderkind. Very few viewers would be likely to come away from this movie without experiencing some sort of emotional reaction.

Munich is a thrilling, highly ambitious political statement, because it declines to demonize and because even the terrorists it portrays show human traits—and because it raises the fundamental question of whether and how democracies should retaliate against terrorists without jeopardizing their own fundamental civil views and ideals.

The leitmotif [theme] reveals itself in two key scenes. In one scene, right at the beginning, Israeli Prime Minister Golda Meir gives the (authentic) order to launch the revenge strike against the Palestinians by uttering this (non-authentic) sentence: "Every civilization repeatedly reaches a point at which it must enter into compromises with its own moral concepts."

In the second central scene, at the end of the film, the disillusioned Israeli secret agent, who killed the Munich murderers, is having another discussion with his boss in New York—and the camera pans across the Manhattan skyline and to the twin towers of the World Trade Center.

Spielberg is telling us that 1972 and 2001 are connected. The message that viewers can take along from the film is that revenge begets revenge and violence begets violence. The greatest enemies in the Middle East aren't the Palestinians or the Israelis, says Spielberg. Instead, the real enemy is "absolute irreconcilability."

There is no question that one can connect the dots from Munich to New York. What began back in 1972 still holds the world in suspense today. The age of international terrorism—complete with aircraft hijackings, hostage-taking and attacks on innocent civilians—began in the early 1970s, when the Vietnam War came to an end and the two superpowers, the United States and the Soviet Union, moved into a stage of détente [lessening of tensions]. It began in the Middle East, and the region remains the epicenter of violence to this day. Yasser Arafat [head of the Palestine Liberation Organization in 1972] chose violence as his method of asserting the Palestinians' claim to their own state, and for him the birth of terrorism was a success. Two years later Arafat, his kuffiya [scarf headdress] on his head and his pistol in his holster, stood before the United Nations and gave a fiery speech about the injustices suffered by the Palestinians—to thunderous applause.

The kidnapping and hostage-taking subsided as Palestinian terror shifted back to its point of origin: the Middle East and the fight against Israel. After all, Arafat's Palestine Liberation Organization, or PLO, had a political goal: an independent Palestinian state.

Osama bin Laden [leader of Al Qaeda responsible for the September 11, 2001, terrorist attacks in the United States] was also an enemy of Israel from the very beginning, calling for liberation of the holy city of Jerusalem and portraying himself as an ardent supporter of the Palestinian cause. But he soon got over his affection for the Palestinians and their cause and has since devoted his attention to the superpowers, first the Soviet Union in Afghanistan and then the United States, on its own soil.

Bin Laden and his ilk have no clear political goal, except perhaps to drive the West out of the Middle East and establish a new caliphate. But this type of Islamism is nothing but a new totalitarianism promoting a backward-looking utopia, a crusade aimed at establishing a theocracy.

Israel's Fight for Survival

Israel is a small country that has been fighting for survival ever since it was established. It will never allow itself to become vulnerable or weak again, and its own security is its highest priority. The Israelis' uncompromising fight against terrorists has served and continues to serve this supreme purpose. In 1972, then Prime Minister Golda Meir told the widows, parents and children of the 11 murdered athletes about her plans for the murderers: "I've decided to pursue each and every one of them. Not one of the people involved in any way will be walking around on this earth for much longer. We will hunt them down until we have killed every last one of them."

The order to kill the assassins was given in the cabinet, writes Israeli author Aaron Klein in his new book *Striking Back*. Cabinet ministers played the roles of judges, the head of the Mossad, acting as a prosecutor, filed the charges and the prime minister (and, later, her successors) pronounced the judgment. Between 1972 and 1992, Israeli intelligence agents in Rome, Paris, Nicosia and Beirut killed more than a dozen Palestinians suspected of having been somehow involved in the Munich incident.

In some cases, the widow of a murdered man would receive an anonymous phone call informing her that a terrorist had met the death he deserved. Officially, however, Israel had nothing to do with the campaign. Democracies can only afford to take their revenge in secret.

Israel continues to assert its right to retribution, responding to deadly attacks in Jerusalem or Tel Aviv with targeted attacks in the Gaza Strip, attacks meant to strike and kill political or military leaders. This "eye for an eye, tooth for a tooth" policy is alive and well in the Middle East today, but it isn't everything.

It's been countered by the 1979 US-sponsored Camp David Peace Treaty between Egyptian President Anwar Sadat and Israeli Prime Minister Menachem Begin. More importantly, it's been countered by the 1993 Oslo Declaration of Principles, under which the PLO and Israel formally recognized one another. Finally, there has been the Israeli withdrawal from the Gaza Strip and from a few settlements in the West Bank, a unilateral step taken by the Israeli government under Prime Minister Ariel Sharon.

> Democracies can be militant, and they can proceed against terrorists without formal declarations of war.

Revenge, Prevention, or Deterrence?

Democracies can be militant, and they can proceed against terrorists without formal declarations of war. In doing so, they inevitably draw the ire of their allies, as has been the case with Israel and the United States. They can persist for some time, but not for very long. And their leaders prefer to call their policies prevention and deterrence, not revenge.

Part of the concept of prevention is the belief that new attacks can be avoided by killing terrorists. This is even a plausible hypothesis, but the problem is that it's virtually impossible to prove. [Islamist groups] Hamas, Hezbollah and al-Qaida may have suffered deadly blows over the years, and even serious setbacks whenever a leading figure was captured or killed, but they have always responded with more acts of terror. Of course, this begs the question as to whether violence doesn't just lead to an escalation of violence. America may have liberated Iraq from [Iraqi dictator Saddam Hussein's] rule, but it has also created many new terrorists.

Despite all efforts at deterrence, democracies almost always make offers to convince terrorists not to engage in terrorism, or at least to weaken them. Prime Minister Sharon may have treated Arafat as the root of all evil, but he was willing to accommodate Arafat's successor, Prime Minister Mahmoud Abbas. Although the hope that Abbas can prevail over such completely irreconcilable groups as Hamas and Islamic Jihad may have disappeared, the fragile hope of peace now rests on Abbas's shoulders.

Even the United States is beginning to show a willingness to negotiate with the Sunni resistance movement in Iraq in an effort to bring it into the democratic process. If this effort were to succeed, it would weaken the resistance movement, a combination of nationalism and terrorism. It appears to be the only way to stem a growing tide of civil war in Iraq. But is that still possible?

In the end, democracies must always hope that the attraction of their own model is stronger than the struggle against it—and that there are some within the ranks of the terrorists who become weary of violence and killing.

Revenge and democracy don't fit together. Democracies thrive from within by domesticating violence. They grow and flourish in times of peace, and they suffer economically in times of militarization. A case in point is the Israelis who supported Sharon's withdrawal from the occupied territories, partly in the hope that their lives would eventually become easier and better as a result.

The United States Faces a Challenge

For democracies, war is an absolute state of emergency, and it's only justified when the democracies themselves are being attacked, when their very existence is at stake.

Democracies become disoriented when they begin lowering civil standards and civil rights—as is the case in the United States today.

Unlike Israel, the United States is a superpower, vastly superior to other countries militarily, incredibly successful economically, and a cultural magnet without equal. America seemed invincible, especially on its own soil. It is precisely for this reason that the shock over the attacks of Sept. 11, 2001, persisted for so long. And it's also for this reason that the Americans allowed their government to use questionable means in its fight against terrorism.

These means include the return of war as a political tool in Afghanistan and Iraq, and they include giving carte blanche to the country's 15 intelligence agencies, whose powers had been systematically limited for good reason ever since Watergate [a scandal involving the Richard Nixon administration]. Since Sept. 11, the CIA is once again allowed to kill, the FBI can enter private homes without a court warrant, the value of civil rights has been diminished, and Guantanamo [prison] has been allowed to exist.

The American democracy, preeminent when it comes to guaranteeing individual constitutional rights, has the nerve to operate pockets of territory where the rule of law no longer applies.

Surprisingly, large portions of what was said and thought within the US government in the days after Sept. 11 are known today. In his book *Bush at War*, Bob Woodward describes how [George W.] Bush, then Secretary of State Colin Powell, Secretary of Defense Donald Rumsfeld and Vice President Richard Cheney, relaxed in their casual clothing, met at bucolic Camp David to review their option. Afghanistan was a no-brainer, but why not take out Saddam Hussein while we're at it? Isn't the Iraqi dictator the spider in the web, and isn't he far more important than Osama bin Laden? What's Syria's role, and how will we deal with Iran?

Then National Security Advisor Condoleezza Rice agreed wholeheartedly. There were, as usual, cheerleaders and there were those with reservations. But the times had changed. The country, edgy and uncharacteristically unified, decided to flip the switch.

Since then the giant US has behaved more like tiny Israel. President Bush has used prevention as his justification for the two wars and the hunt for al-Qaida, taking the war to wherever the terrorists presumably lived, were given shelter and were nurtured, so that America would never have to accept another 9/11 again. Osama bin Laden lost his base in Afghanistan and was forced to regroup. . . .

Spielberg as "Guardian of Public Morals?"

Steven Spielberg is an American patriot and a friend of Israel. *Munich* deals skeptically with the right of revenge, and the film is a semi-distanced commentary on contemporary terrorism. It raises questions to which there are no easy answers. At times, the film comes across almost as the brooding product of a European director.

But Spielberg is Hollywood, and although Hollywood may want to encourage its paying viewers to engage in some contemplation, it certainly has no intention of troubling them with unambiguous political messages.

By making a political film, Spielberg has put himself in the line of fire. He has made enemies, not just among columnists from New York to Jerusalem, but also among the families of the 11 victims of Munich, to whom Spielberg also plans to raise a monument, and among the Mossad avengers whom he elevates to the status of tragic heroes in the film.

Ankie Spitzer, 59, the widow of André Spitzer, a fencing trainer murdered in Munich, speaks on behalf of the victims.

Ankie Spitzer, the widow of the Israeli fencing coach, visits the room in the Olympic Village where the hostages were held and two were killed—including her husband. (© **AP Photo.**)

She insisted on visiting the scene of the murders. She wanted to see the images that were in André's head when he died. Although she has long since remarried, and now has three children with her second husband, Spitzer has not forgotten anything or forgiven anyone. Today Spitzer (she kept her murdered husband's last name) works as the Israel correspondent for a Dutch television station.

When she found out that *Munich* was being filmed, Spitzer called Spielberg's office to offer the director her advice, but she was quickly sent packing by the director's gatekeepers. Spielberg later found out about it, apologized and arranged a private screening for Spitzer and other family members of the victims. The widow of André Spitzer gives the film a mixed review: "As long as it's telling the story of Munich, the film is realistic and sensitive. But the story that follows is mostly made-up—Spielberg apparently sees himself as a sort of guardian of public morals for the nation."

What Spitzer means by "the story that follows" is Spielberg's fictionalization of the facts, which he uses to transform the cold-blooded agents into brooding men and give faces and emotions to the terrorists.

Mike Harari, 78, the former head of the commando units Mossad had assembled for its crusade of revenge, speaks on behalf of the avengers. Mossad's campaign, appropriately enough, was dubbed "Wrath of God."

Mossad later sent Harari to Panama, where he developed an elite unit for then dictator Manuel Noriega, still on the White House's good side at the time. But in December 1989, when Washington's view of Noriega changed and the US was about to launch its invasion, Harari disappeared. Information he provided presumably helped ensure that Noriega, the country's drug- and weapons-dealing dictator, ended up in an American prison.

Harari's reputation is shot at Mossad these days. The retiree lives like a recluse in his house near Tel Aviv, and for years Harari refused to give interviews. But when Spielberg's film began to make waves, he was suddenly back in the news, telling the press that "no one from Spielberg's team contacted me—what a shame."

No Neat Hollywood Ending

Harari's and Spitzer's objections to the film are understandable, as is Spielberg's somewhat blithe treatment of both the facts and advisors. A few years earlier, two documentary filmmakers conducted extensive interviews of the victims, the avengers and the assassins. Arthur Cohn and Kevin MacDonald were awarded the Oscar in 2000 for their moving documentary, *One Day in September*.

The historical truth is mixed. Harari's commando unit killed a number of secondary figures, as well as two key players behind the Munich attack: Atif Bseisu was a member of the innermost circle of Abu Iyad, the head of Black September, while Ali Hassan Salameh was the commander of Arafat's bodyguards. Iyad himself died at the hands of one of his own bodyguards in 1991.

Three of the eight assassins survived the shootout in Fürstenfeldbruck. And what about justice? After they had spent exactly 53 days in German prisons, the German government swapped the men for 13 passengers and 7 crew members of a hijacked Lufthansa aircraft. The rumor that the West German government in Bonn had entered into a deal of sorts with the Palestinians in connection with this incident—Bonn's release of the Palestinian terrorists in exchange for a promise of no further hijackings of German planes—has never quite gone away, and it's also supported by a few important star witnesses.

> Appalling attacks like Munich 1972 and New York 2001 inescapably trigger thoughts of violent revenge.

Hans-Jochen Vogel, the doyen of Germany's Social Democratic Party (SPD), says that whenever former Chancellor Willy Brandt was asked why he gave in to the terrorists so quickly in the Lufthansa hijacking incident, he would say nothing and merely shrug his shoulders. In Cohn's documentary Ulrich Wegener, who, after Munich, established the elite GSG-9 unit—which was to make up for everything that went wrong in Munich when it successfully liberated a terrorist-held Lufthansa jet in Mogadishu in 1977—says that he believes there was an agreement with the Palestinians.

At least one of the three Munich murderers, Jamal al-Gashey, survived somewhere in Africa. The Mossad commandos never managed to catch him or Abu Daud, the mastermind behind the Olympic attack. He became a pacifist and presumably lives in Syria today.

Appalling attacks like Munich 1972 and New York 2001 inescapably trigger thoughts of violent revenge. But the "Wrath of God," carried out by human hands, remains by necessity incomplete.

Abu Daoud: No Regrets for Munich Olympics

Associated Press

The following viewpoint relays part of a 2006 interview with Abu Daoud, the Palestinian guerilla leader who planned the terrorist attack on the Munich Olympics in 1972. Daoud (whose given name was Mohammed Oudeh and who died of natural causes in 2010) lived at the time in Syria, the only country that would allow him entry. In the interview Daoud describes the ideas behind the attack as well as general preparations for it. He argues that there were no plans for any killing and that the attackers hoped to exchange their hostages for Palestinians held in Israeli jails. But even though the attack turned out badly, Daoud claims, it was a victory nonetheless. It brought the world's attention to the Palestinian cause, taking advantage of one of the few weapons that Palestinians possessed.

M ohammed Oudeh is old and stooped, his hair and mustache gray. It is difficult to imagine him as Abu Daoud, the key planner of the assault on the 1972 Munich Olympics that left 11 Israeli athletes dead.

But the 69-year-old former guerrilla leader is as militant as ever: In an interview with The Associated Press, he recounts how PLO leaders—angry that the Palestinians were denied an Olympic slot—dreamed up the attack while sitting at a sidewalk cafe in Rome.

And he shows no regret.

Discussing the Palestinians' struggle for a homeland and rejecting the use of the word "terrorist" to describe its fighters, he said of the Munich days: "There was nothing we weren't prepared to do to keep the Palestinian cause in the public eye."

"Before Munich, we were simply terrorists. After Munich, at least people started asking who are these terrorists? What do they want? Before Munich, nobody had the slightest idea about Palestine," he said.

He insists Israel must make concessions if it ever wants peace.

'Today, I cannot fight you anymore, but my grandson will and his grandsons, too.'

"Today, I cannot fight you anymore, but my grandson will and his grandsons, too," Abu Daoud said, addressing Israelis.

Director Steven Spielberg's movie Munich has revived discussions of the Sept. 5, 1972, hostage-taking that shocked the world. Abu Daoud, who did not participate in the attack itself, has not seen the film, but has read about it and hopes someday to see it on DVD.

The movie focuses on the Israeli Mossad intelligence agency's actions to hunt down and kill those it believed responsible for the assault on the Munich Olympic village by members of Abu Daoud's "Black September" group. The group was a violent offshoot of the mainstream

Palestinian Fatah faction, and staged attacks on Israelis in Europe in the 1970s.

Two Israeli athletes were killed in the assault, and nine others died in a botched rescue attempt by the German police. A German policeman and five Palestinian gunmen also were killed.

Abu Daoud first acknowledged having a role in the Munich operation in a 1999 book, *Palestine: From Jerusalem to Munich*, that caused an uproar when it came out.

After the 1972 attack, he lived in eastern Europe and then in Lebanon until civil war broke out in 1975. He went to Jordan, and from there to Ramallah in the West Bank in 1993 after the Palestinians' Oslo peace accords with Israel.

But when Abu Daoud's book came out in 1999, he was banned from returning to Ramallah after a trip to Jordan, and finally settled in Syria—the only country that would take him.

He agreed to be interviewed by the AP at a Damascus hospital where he said he was having a checkup.

Talking about the 1972 attack, Abu Daoud recalled sitting at a cafe in Rome with fellow PLO guerrilla leader Abu Iyad and his assistant, Mohammed al-Omari, when they read in a newspaper that the International Olympics Committee had refused the PLO's request to send a Palestinian delegation to the Munich Olympics.

Morale was already sagging after the PLO's humiliating retreat from Jordan, where the late King Hussein had crushed Palestinian guerrillas.

"I remember Abu Iyad looked at me and said: 'Let's participate in the Olympics in our own way. Let's kidnap (Israeli) hostages and swap them for prisoners in Israel,'" Abu Daoud said.

Abu Daoud said he immediately took to the idea, and was given the task of doing the operation's groundwork. After several reconnaissance missions to Munich, it was

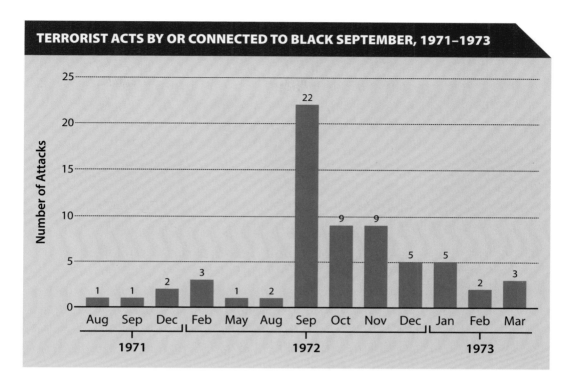

TERRORIST ACTS BY OR CONNECTED TO BLACK SEPTEMBER, 1971–1973

agreed that eight masked gunmen would storm the Israeli athletes' dormitory and take them hostage.

He said that 10 days before the attack, he went to Munich again and took from Abu Iyad weapons, mainly Kalashnikov assault rifles, that had been smuggled in.

On the night of the attack, Abu Daoud said he took the eight attackers to dinner in a restaurant at the Munich train station, then the group got taxis for the Olympic Village. They carried their weapons in sports bags.

The plan was to cut through the fence and break in. But when the group arrived, the eight attackers were able to mingle with drunken American athletes who were climbing over a fence, Abu Daoud said. Inside the dormitory, the gunmen put on masks and began their assault. Abu Daoud, who had stayed at the fence, slipped away.

He said he had no qualms about the operation because he considered the Israeli athletes, as military

Supporters of Abu Daoud carry his coffin toward the Palestinian Martyrs' Cemetery on the outskirts of Damascus, Syria, in 2010. The mastermind behind the Munich massacre believed it to have been a success because it brought the Palestinian cause to the world's attention. (© **Louai Beshara/AFP/Getty Images.**)

reservists, legitimate targets. But he said the intent was not to kill the Israelis but to use them as bargaining chips to free more than 200 Palestinians jailed in Israel.

"We had strict orders not to kill anyone except in self defense," he said.

Things did not go as planned. Two athletes resisted the gunmen and were fatally shot, and Israeli Prime Minister Golda Meir refused to negotiate. By the time the standoff ended 21 hours later in the German rescue attempt, 17 people were dead.

Still, the Palestinians considered it a victory.

"Through Munich, we were able to force our cause into the homes of 500 million people," Abu Daoud said.

Abu Daoud himself almost died in what he believes was a Mossad attack. In 1981, as he sat in a hotel cafe in Warsaw, Poland, a gunman fired on him, hitting Abu Daoud in his left wrist, chest, stomach and jaw.

"It was a Palestinian double agent, recruited by the Mossad. . . . He was arrested 10 years later, put on trial (by the PLO) and executed," Abu Daoud said. It was not possible to verify his account.

Abu Daoud watches Palestinian events closely, including the election victory by the militant group Hamas.

He said he is opposed "in principle" to suicide bombings.

"But then I remind myself that the Palestinians have nothing else to fight with. We have absolutely nothing while our enemy is armed to the teeth. How can you face such an enemy with all its might, if you don't use unconventional and illogical means?" he said.

> 'We have absolutely nothing while our enemy [Israel] is armed to the teeth. How can you face such an enemy with all its might, if you don't use unconventional and illogical means?'

"In Fatah, we were a bit lenient and ready to give a little. The Israelis didn't want to give anything in return. Now they have Hamas. If they (Israelis) don't give them something, someone even harsher than Hamas will emerge," Abu Daoud said.

"This is the logic of history."

CHAPTER 3

Personal Narratives

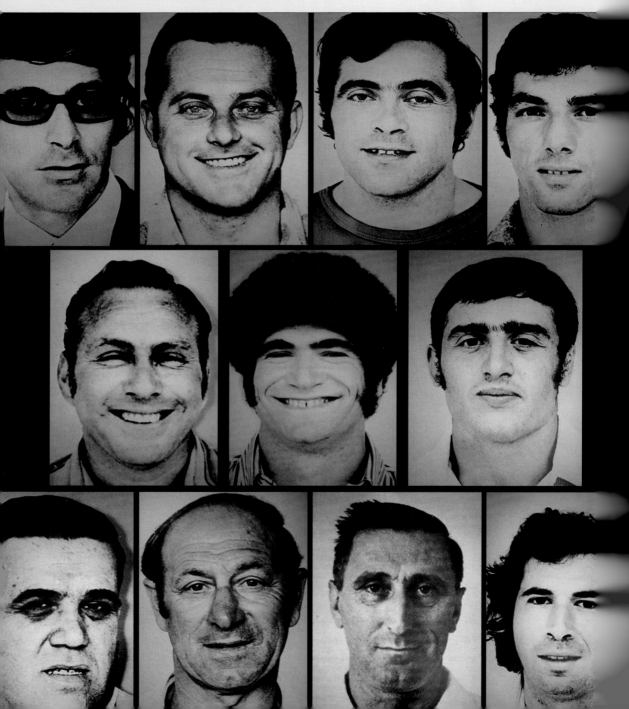

A Survivor Remembers and Draws Lessons from the Tragedy of the Munich Massacre

Yau Ng

In the following viewpoint, written by reporter Yau Ng and published in the *Daily Pennsylvanian,* the student newspaper at the University of Pennsylvania, Israeli fencer Dan Alon recalls the Munich Massacre. Alon was one of the Israeli athletes housed in an apartment that the Black September terrorists did not storm. As he recounts during a visit to the university in 1976, he and others were able to escape despite terrorist gunfire. He and the other survivors ultimately accompanied the bodies of the victims as they were returned to Israel, and they did not take part in any further competitions after the massacre on September 5, 1972.

A photo collage shows the eleven Israeli men killed during the 1972 Munich Olympics Massacre. (© Timur Emek/dapd/AP Photo.)

At about 5:30 A.M. on Sept. 5, 1972, Dan Alon awoke to the sound of machine guns and a bullet ripping through the wall of his apartment, just behind his bed.

The Israeli fencer—who survived the 1972 Munich Olympics massacre—addressed around 250 people on Friday [November 3, 2006] in the Terrace Room of Logan Hall [at the University of Pennsylvania], giving a personal account of what he called one of the "worst acts of terror in history."

During the massacre, Palestinian militants took hostages from two of three Israeli apartments, and eventually killed 11 athletes. Alon was in the apartment that was not attacked.

He said, however, that he was able to see the attackers when he looked down through a window at the entrance to his apartment and spotted a man in a white hat, armed with a machine gun and a hand grenade, talking to a policeman.

After overhearing that conversation, Alon said he gathered that Palestinians from the group Black Septem-

The surviving members of the Israeli delegation to the 1972 Munich Olympic Games prepares to board a special El Al flight to Israel on September 7, 1972. (© AFP/Getty Images.)

ber had taken Israeli athletes from two of the apartments, and that two of his friends had been killed.

A Risky Escape

Figuring that they would be attacked next, Alon said that he and the other members of his apartment jumped over the balcony and sprinted away. He said they miraculously succeeded, even though the Black September militants opened fire on them.

"When my friends and I returned the next day to the Israeli residence to pack our friends' belongings, there was blood everywhere," Alon said. "The saddest thing was collecting the toys that our friends had bought for their children."

He said, however, that the group did not let the deaths affect the sense of camaraderie of the team.

"Then we went home with 11 coffins," he said. "We arrived as a delegation, and we returned as a delegation. Always a delegation."

Alon quit fencing competitively after that because he was disappointed in the ideal that the Olympics stood for. "It represented friendship, peace, and unity between nations. It didn't matter that we were from Israel, athletes from other nations were friendly to us," he said.

Alon also said that he was happy that [film director] Steven Spielberg had made these events into the movie *Munich* because he does not want people to forget what happened that day. In that vein, he noted that he knew many young people who had never heard of the massacre.

> 'This act of terror during the Olympics was not part of a war between Israel and terror; it is actually part of a war between the world and terror.'

"We need to understand that this act of terror during the Olympics was not part of a war between Israel and terror; it is actually part of a war between the world and terror," he said at the end of his speech.

An Israeli Athlete Remembers the Day He Lost His Teammates

Joseph Santoliquito

The Jewish Community Centers Association of North America holds a series of athletic competitions for young people every year. These events are known as the Maccabi Games, named in part to commemorate a Jewish rebel from Biblical times. In 2011 some of the games were held at Villanova University in Pennsylvania, where a survivor of the Munich attack, wrestler Alon Howard, spoke before a gathering of athletes and their supporters. The following viewpoint was written by Joseph Santoliquito, a reporter for a local newspaper. Howard was lucky because, as a wrestler, he ordinarily would have stayed in the apartment attacked by the terrorists. But on the night of September 4, 1972, he was staying with a friend in another apartment instead. In his Villanova talk, Howard describes some of the feelings he and other survivors experienced as the attack unfolded, focusing on his memories of murdered wrestling coach Moshe Weinberg.

SOURCE. Joseph Santoliquito, "Maccabi Games Guest Remembers Teammates Killed at Munich Olympics," *Roxborough-Manayunk Patch,* August 19, 2011. Copyright © 2011 by Patch.com. All rights reserved. Reproduced by permission.

On Sept. 5, 1972, in Munich, Germany, 17-year-old Israeli junior Olympian Alon Howard escaped violent death by sheer luck.

He will never forget that 11 others on his team did not.

"They're all dead," Howard heard as he awoke the next morning.

The former flyweight wrestler told the 1,200 young Jewish athletes at this week's Main Line-Philadelphia JCC Maccabi Games [an athletic event for young people sponsored by the Jewish Community Centers Association of North America] to never forget the 11 Israelis massacred at the Munich Olympics by the terrorist group Black September. At Sunday's opening ceremonies in Villanova University's Pavilion, he also sat down for an interview with *Patch* to describe the confusion and anguish he and the other surviving Israeli team members endured.

"The morning it happened, the Munich police came to us and told us what happened. They wanted to make sure we were protected. We were told a lot of conflicting things as it was going on, and I remember later that night, Sept. 5, we were told that they were rescued," Howard told *Patch*. "Then that next morning, I remember waking up and someone said, 'They're all dead.' That's how we were woken up the next day. I can never forget that."

The flyweight wrestler had slept at a friend's apartment in the Olympic complex the night of Sept. 4, rather than in the Israeli national team quarters as wrestling coach Moshe Weinberg—virtually a second father to Howard—had invited him to do.

Remembering Coach Weinberg

"I was traveling with a friend from the Israeli youth team and Moshe wanted me to stay with the Olympic team that night," Howard told *Patch*. "I was young, 17 with hopes of competing for the Olympic team in 1976. Moshe was like a father to me. He was my coach and very close friend. He was someone who cared about sports and the athletes he coached. I remember telling Moshe that I was with a friend of mine and I would meet him the next morning. He wasn't there."

Howard found out the morning of Sept. 5 about the eight Palestinian terrorists that infiltrated the Olympic Village carrying machine guns in duffel bags. They broke into the apartment complex where Israeli coaches were staying, and were confronted by Weinberg. He tried bat-

Israeli athletes attend a 2002 ceremony at the monument to the victims of the massacre outside Munich's Olympic Stadium. (© Damien Meyer/ AFP/Getty Images.)

tling the terrorists, before he was shot in the face and forced to find more hostages at gunpoint.

It was Weinberg who led the terrorists to the apartment that housed the weightlifters and wrestlers, hoping they could combat the terrorists. But the six wrestlers and weightlifters were asleep and caught by surprise.

As the Israelis were being led from one apartment to another down the spiral staircase of the building, Weinberg fought back again, allowing wrestler Gad Tsobari to escape through an underground parking garage, before being shot again and killed. Weightlifter Yossef Romano, an Israeli soldier in the Six-Day War, attacked another terrorist and was also shot and killed.

"I think about those days all of the time," Howard said. "I have pictures of Moshe and I'm very close to his family to this day. Moshe had a three-month-old son that he would never see again. Moshe was an amazing person, and he deserves to be remembered. It's why it was important for me to be here at the ceremonies for this."

Howard returned to Israel with his slain teammates in the belly of the plane. He moved to the United States in 1977—now living in Huntington Valley, Montgomery County, with his wife and three children—and he has an Olympic portrait of the 11 victims hanging in his living room, looking toward the heavens.

'It's an important part of Jewish history and an important part of history for everyone that we should never forget.'

"It's an important part of Jewish history and an important part of history for everyone that we should never forget," Howard said. "We can never forget."

An Israeli Wrestler and His Family: From the Soviet Union to Israel to Munich

Ronen Dorfan

Some of the Israeli athletes murdered at Munich originally came from somewhere else—not surprising since Israel was such a new nation. Weightlifter David Berger, for example, was from Cleveland, Ohio, and his parents still lived there at the time of Berger's death. Another example was wrestler Mark Slavin, the subject of the following viewpoint by Israeli sportswriter Ronen Dorfan. Slavin originally came from Ukraine in the Soviet Union. He chose to emigrate to get away from the anti-Semitism he claimed to see around him in the former Communist empire, moving to Israel to pursue his athletic ambitions. Much of his family ended up joining him. The viewpoint traces Slavin's arrival in Israel, his inclusion on the

SOURCE. Ronen Dorfan, "Nearly 40 Years After Terror at Munich Olympics, a Fallen Legend Still Shines, " *The PostGame Yahoo,* September 5, 2011. Copyright © 2011 by Ronen Dorfan. All rights reserved. Reproduced by permission.

1972 Olympic team, and his death in the eventual tragedy. Dorfan also notes the sad effect that Slavin's death had on his immigrant family members.

There is one definite theme that repeats itself in all the clear or vague recollections of people who remember the great Mark Slavin in his wrestling years in [the Soviet city of] Minsk. No one remembers a child. No one remembers a teenager. The boy, who at the age of 12 had the physical strength of a grown man, matured in wisdom and thoughtfulness and purpose way beyond his years.

In a family dominated by women, he became a leader. Chopping firewood with a great axe in autumn, speaking passionately and decisively against the institutional anti-Semitism they confronted in the tense political climate of the early 1970s, drawing dozens of friends and admirers to the family home and leading them in song with his red accordion.

Today, when Mark's sister, Olga, takes his clothes out of the closet every now and then to air them out a little, she is often surprised. They seem so small. In reality, Mark was a wrestler in the 74kg division—163 pounds—but she remembers him as a giant. Ten years her elder, he would not once hold her hand but would always carry her on his broad shoulders. With him she would encounter the world not from street-level, but riding a mythical titan.

From the perspective of time, she can see things she could not have appreciated as a child. She once found an old psychology book among his belongings. What did a carefree superstar athlete of the Soviet Republic find in what was considered a suspiciously bourgeois field?

Few of his loved ones ever saw him compete. In his free afternoons, [Slavin's brother] Elik would visit the Sports Palace. Soaking in pride, he heard the spontaneous whistles and cheers as Mark's speed and power amazed all spectators. They marveled at the ease with which he would grind opponents—fellow students at first, then soon established Olympic-level competitors.

> Mark began to acknowledge that anti-Semitism was deep-rooted even in the supposedly open and democratic world of sport.

But his family could never attend the big competitions. These were held in faraway parts of the giant republic. Glory came in the form of an excited phone call, a radio bulletin or a newspaper headline. Like in 1971, when Mark returned from the Ukraine as Junior champion of the Republic. Or later, when he achieved an improbable draw with Viktor Igumenov, the reigning six-time world champion.

In his years at the Sports Palace, Mark developed an abhorrence of Soviet-Russian culture. He grew closer to his paternal grandfather Zalman, who would tell him of the Hebrew classes he had taught before the war, classes that now were forbidden. Zalman talked about his sadness on not being able to hold a Bar Mitzvah for his grandchildren.

A New Realization

Mark began to acknowledge that anti-Semitism was deep-rooted even in the supposedly open and democratic world of sport. A dramatic decision began building up inside him. Soon after his 18th birthday, he filed a request for a visa to Israel. He would not represent the Soviet Union. He would relinquish the elite status the Soviet Union had afforded him. He would refuse an apartment, scholarship, international travel and handsome salary offered to him if he was to cancel his visa request. This was tantamount to treason.

He intended to emigrate alone, but his decision inspired the family. Grandmother Chasya, for whom he was always a son, decided the whole family would join him. They were a group of 17 people on a cold morning at Minsk's central railway station, boarding a train to Vienna.

KGB [Soviet secret police] officers patrolled the station, taking note of people coming to bid the traitor farewell. Nevertheless, several of Minsk's Jewish athletes and other friends defied the danger and came. Michael Mirsky brought his champion student an oil-painting. They were to leave an entire life behind. [Little sister] Olga was allowed but one small rubber doll to take with her.

Mark hardly spoke through the entire journey as the train crossed Poland and Czechoslovakia en route to the West. He sat quietly next to Elik. His aunt Masha remembers him shining, as if an aura surrounded him.

From Tel Aviv to Munich, 1972

On his first day in Israel, Mark went to the "Hapoel Tel Aviv" Wrestling division. It was the only Israeli wrestling club he had heard of. He told the club officials he was the Junior Champion of the USSR [Union of Soviet Socialist Republics].

Quick bouts were organized to verify his extraordinary pedigree. He hardly broke a sweat in defeating experienced wrestlers from any weight division. As a final test, an Olympic medalist from France, Daniel Robin, was flown into Israel. Mark beat him with ease.

As he boarded the plane to the Olympics, he promised Elik to bring home a medal—to tear it away from the Soviets.

On 25th August 1972, Mark Slavin wrote a letter from Munich:

> As he boarded the plane to the Olympics, he promised . . . to bring home a medal—to tear it away from the Soviets.

Father, Mother, Granny, Elik, Ola and my two aunts. I hope you have a happy new year and that you will all be happy and healthy.

I am writing to you from the Olympic village. It is a place of the future. I cannot stop staring at it. They tell us that in the future, in 100–150 years, they will build cities like this—with cars only traveling underground.

We arrived safely. We had a tour of Switzerland before we arrived that was very beautiful. We were given a luxurious room. They bought us Adidas shoes and tracksuits, half price, I think I will buy for father and Elik.

Athletes from many countries are living with us. I exchanged pins with them. Only the Soviet Union hasn't arrived. When they come I will meet everyone.

In the meantime I am training once a day.

I received 300 Deutschmarks but I won't waste it on nonsense. I wrote grandpa Zalman a letter. I didn't 't say anything. Like a Soviet athlete writing to his grandfather.

Today we will go to the synagogue to pray. I will pray for all the Jews to get to Israel and fulfill their dream, like I did. I pray for uncles Isa and Misha to emigrate too; though I understand there is no news on their case.

Regards to all,

Mark

Goodbye, 1972

In the days leading up to competition, Mark trained with Bert Kops, a Dutch wrestler in the 90 kg division. They were also training with Petros Galaktopoulos, the eventual silver medalist in Mark's division. Kops had never heard of Mark Slavin and was surprised that the almost anonymous Israel had such a wrestler. He later learned he was a Soviet champion and now it made more sense to him. They never actually spoke as they had no common language.

He felt this was a wrestler with power and purpose from another sphere, way superior even to Galaktopoulos —a wrestler of considerable fame. He sensed the resolve of an athlete about to do something big. He was convinced he was going to win a medal—very possibly the gold.

On the morning of September 5, 1972, [Slavin's parents] Anna and Jacob went to the bank. It was the day Mark was due to compete at the Olympics. They hardly knew a word of Hebrew, but Anna noticed a sports paper at the newsstand outside the bank.

She identified a large photo of Moshe Weinberg, the wrestling coach. It seemed odd. Why would the newspaper carry the photo of the coach and not the athlete? She knew one of the bank clerks that spoke Yiddish. She asked him why.

In the early hours of September 5th, 1972, a group of eight terrorists from the Palestinian "Black September" faction entered 31 Connollystrasse—the Israeli team residence at the Olympic Village. They killed two team members, including Mark's coach, Moshe Weinberg, and took nine hostages, Mark Slavin among them.

An 18-hour standoff was followed by a failed ambush and rescue attempt by the German police at a local air base. All of the hostages died.

In years to come, the Israeli intelligence agency Mossad and the Israeli Defense Force [IDF] special units hunted down and killed dozens of those involved in planning and carrying out the massacre. The operations included one mistaken assassination of a Moroccan waiter in Norway.

> " When Mark Slavin died in Munich, the family's extraordinary strength . . . was lost as well. "

The Olympic Games in Munich commenced on the 6th of September following a memorial service at the Olympic Stadium. A relative of one of the victims died of a heart attack during the service.

A Family's Pain

When Mark Slavin died in Munich, the family's extraordinary strength that saw them through hardship from [World War II battle-site] Stalingrad to Israel was lost as well. At his funeral, [grandmother] Chasya pointed at a small strip of land and asked to be buried there, beside the child she had breastfed. Within two years, she is granted her wish; she died at the age of 59.

Anna and Jacob became sick, heartbroken people for the rest of their days. They could not find the courage to send their own children on school trips. Anna would suffer anxiety attacks even to the sound of Arabic from the television. She imagined the last sounds of her son's life.

When Elik went to war in Lebanon with the IDF, he received the kerchief that had saved his grandfather in Stalingrad [during World War II]. He survived the war. Somehow, despite serving in a commando unit, danger was always five minutes or a few kilometers away. He often wondered if the cloth should have gone to Munich with Mark. But how were they to know?

Like his father, Elik believes Mark never kissed a girl. A few years after his death, Jacob candidly told a BBC journalist that his son died a virgin. Elik knows his brother showed interest in a girl he had met at the Wingate Sports Institute north of Tel Aviv, intending to court her after the Games.

But Olga saw a woman at the memorial services. She came year after year. Brown haired. Nice. She wants to believe this was Mark's lover, but she could never ask her parents. Never enquire. They would not talk.

In Minsk [now in independent Belarus], Aunt Genia could not mourn in public. The house was still under KGB surveillance. She went visiting family friends to listen to their stories about a boy who at 18 was a hero to Minsk's Jewish Community. During one of these visits, her son David was playing with fire, got injured and hospitalized. The foreign press mistakenly reported it was a result of anti-Semitic attacks.

In Zhlobin, the [family's] ancestral hometown, Zalman Slavin received the letter his grandson promised to write him from Munich. The once large Jewish community had diminished to only 500 people after the Holocaust. The fact that one of the dead Olympians had ties to the town was not published, for fear of anti-Semitic attacks. The town synagogue had long been confiscated by the authorities and Zalman organized prayers at a friend's home.

Eyewitness at Munich

Dwight Chapin

In the following viewpoint, written in 2005, sportswriter Dwight Chapin recounts his experiences and reactions during the 1972 Munich massacre. In town to cover the Olympics for the *Los Angeles Times,* Chapin found himself acting as a political reporter as well as a sports journalist. He recalls that, once the decision was reached to continue the games, the last days of the event were quiet and even fearful; participants were unsure whether another attack might be possible. The Munich Olympics came to a close in strong contrast to what West Germans had hoped would be remembered as the "Games of Peace and Joy" or the "Happy Games."

It's a memory that's still very close to the surface, even after more than three decades, a memory that can be triggered by a single word:

Munich.

That's the title of a new Steven Spielberg movie, but, for me, it will always symbolize something that has nothing to do with celluloid, something very real—events so powerful they've never left my consciousness.

SOURCE. Dwight Chapin, "Eyewitness at Munich," *San Francisco Chronicle,* December 18, 2005. Copyright © 2005 by San Francisco Chronicle. All rights reserved. Reproduced by permission.

In the late summer of 1972, I was the only sports reporter covering the Munich Olympic Games for the *Los Angeles Times,* along with the noted columnist Jim Murray.

I'd had my hands full in Germany for a couple of weeks. It was all sports, all the time, story after story, day after day, food and sleep very much afterthoughts. But my bosses back in California always wanted more. Which is why, on a scheduled off day for track and field competition, Sept. 5, I decided to get up very early and catch the subway to downtown Munich to gather material for a profile of the old German city my editors wanted.

In the early afternoon, I stopped at a cafe for a cup of coffee and noticed a man at the next table holding a French newspaper with a huge headline that said "MORT!" and a photograph of what looked like bodies lying in the Olympic village. I rushed outside and bought my own copy of the newspaper. But my knowledge of French was minimal, and I still was confused about exactly what had happened.

But I could tell that these Olympics were now about much more than fun and games.

I hurried back to the press center to look for my colleague Murray and try to fill in the missing pieces, but he wasn't there. He had gotten into the cordoned-off Olympic village, to the building at 31 Connollystrasse where terrorists in stocking masks had killed two Israeli athletes and were now negotiating with a German government official over the fate of nine hostages.

I found out that Joe Alex Morris, the *Times'* bureau chief in Bonn, had been brought in to handle the breaking news, and I scrambled to help him, digging whatever information I could out of what had turned into an armed camp.

Throughout the Games, the Germans had bent over backward to try to erase the memories of Nazi militarism and show a benign image to the world, starting with the release of a flock of white doves at the opening ceremony.

The German police at the Olympic site wore light blue uniforms and white caps, which, Murray wrote, made them look "like English schoolboys going out punting on the Thames with a wicker basket full of watercress sandwiches."

But they were dressed very differently when I got back to the Olympic village that day. They wore military garb and World War II-style steel helmets, and they had thrown up barbed wire all around the perimeter. There were tanks, machine guns and armed troops everywhere. The peaceful celebration clearly was over. Jewish blood had again been spilled on German soil, if not by German hands this time.

> The peaceful celebration clearly was over. Jewish blood had again been spilled on German soil, if not by German hands this time.

The Palestinian terrorists—a group calling itself Black September—ultimately demanded the release of 200 prisoners from Israeli jails and safe passage out of Germany for themselves, but that didn't happen. At the Munich airport, three of them were killed by sharpshooters, and, in a subsequent gunbattle, the nine hostages, two more terrorists and a police officer died.

Olympic organizers dithered as to what to do about resuming the Games. Nothing happened for 12 hours after the first Israelis were murdered, and, finally, competition was halted for only a day.

Everywhere in the Olympic village, before the decision to keep going had been made, there were impromptu meetings, people agonizing, trying to make sense of what had happened. Some athletes favored calling off the rest of the Games, out of respect for the slain Israelis and the potential for more trouble, others didn't. Many weren't sure.

One of the most memorable sights was U.S. distance runner Kenny Moore—tall, thin, almost Christlike in appearance—standing with a swarm of reporters around him, and saying perhaps everyone should go back to competition in plain white uniforms rather than nationalistic symbols.

But the Olympic organizers, mindful of the money that was at stake as well as the Games' future, never considered anything like that. Later that day, at a memorial service in the track stadium attended by 80,000 people—many of them softly crying—84-year-old Avery Brundage, who was in his final days as International Olympic Committee chief, ranted about pressure from African blacks a few days earlier that resulted in Rhodesia's expulsion from the Olympics and railed against the commercialism of athletes endorsing tennis shoes. His stark insensitivity that day remains vivid.

And then Brundage spoke the words that still ring in many ears, including mine.

"The Games," he said, "must go on."

The route back from the track stadium to the press dormitories went through the Olympic village. I detoured briefly to 31 Connollystrasse, where a bank of cut flowers now ran the entire length of the building—a beautiful profusion of colors in front of the place that had become the focal point of Black September.

The emotion, the anger I'd felt through much of Brundage's speech at the memorial service, came out in a flood of tears that made me feel better, but not much.

> The mood everywhere was somber in the last few days of the Munich Olympics.

The mood everywhere was somber in the last few days of the Munich Olympics. There was fear surrounding what was left of the competition, uncertainty about what might come next. Like a number of other reporters, I covered the closing ceremony from a television set in the press center rather than go to the stadium.

After writing that story, exhaustion finally overtook me. The day after the Games ended, I sought some needed peace and solace in a small hotel on the outskirts of Munich. There was a neighborhood bar on the corner, and while I was drinking a beer there that night, a group of Germans at a nearby table invited me to join them.

After a round or two, one of the men, who spoke only German, insisted that one of his friends who knew English apologize to me—an American—for what the Germans had done in World War II.

I asked how old the man was. He was the same age as me. We both had been 7 when the war ended. That he was too young to have borne any responsibility for it didn't matter to him. Not with this sad, new shadow over his country, a shadow that seemingly no one—least of all the Germans—saw coming.

1896   The Olympic Games, an institution in ancient Greece, are revived after 2,500 years. Advocates praise the Greek idea that sports could take the place of political competition or even warfare and increase international understanding.

1936   The Summer Olympic Games are held in Berlin, Germany, then the capital of Adolf Hitler's Nazi Germany. Some Jewish athletes boycott the games.

1939–1945   During World War II, Nazi Germany massacres about six million European Jews before Hitler's regime is finally crushed.

1948   The country of Israel is founded as the modern Jewish state.

1948–1949   Many Palestinian Arabs are uprooted due to the various agreements that create Israel. Many become stateless refugees, unwelcome in both Israel and neighboring Arab countries.

1967   In the Six Day War, Israel defeats a coalition of Arab nations and greatly expands its territory, which creates new groups of Palestinian refugees.

1968–1969   Founded in 1964, the Palestine Liberation Organization (PLO) grows and becomes increasingly independent of sponsorship from Arab nations. It engages in small-scale attacks against Israel, a tactic favored by Yasser Arafat, leader of the Fatah wing of the PLO.

1969–1970 The PLO and Kingdom of Jordan fight a low-level "war of attrition" against Israel, involving both attacks on Israeli communities and reprisals against PLO attacks in Jordan.

1970 King Hussein of Jordan moves to end PLO influence in his country after a series of attacks and airplane hijackings, resulting in both violence against refugees and the expulsion of the PLO as an organization. In response, members of Fatah and other groups form a splinter group known as Black September.

1971 November 28: Black September assassinates the Jordanian prime minister in Cairo, Egypt.

December: Black September launches further attacks on Jordanian officials inEurope. These European incidents continue into 1972.

1972 May 8: Black September hijacks a passenger airliner owned by Sabena, the Belgian airline. The plane and its passengers are flown to an Israeli airport, where the hijackers hope to exchange the passengers for Palestinians in Israeli jails. An Israeli commando team eventually ends the incident, killing two of the four hijackers and arresting the others. All passengers are rescued.

August 26: The Summer Olympic Games begin in Munich, West Germany. They are the first Olympics to be held in Germany since the "Nazi Olympics" in 1936. Israel sends a team of fifteen athletes accompanied by coaches and other officials.

September 5: Black September enter the Munich Olympic Village at 4:30 A.M. The massacre ends fifteen hours later with a shootout at the Fürstenfeldbruck airfield, a military base outside Munich.

September 6: A memorial service, attended by three thousand athletes and eighty thousand spectators, is held at the Munich Olympic Stadium as the competition is suspended for one day. Remaining Israeli athletes leave Munich.

September 8: Israel bombs eight PLO bases in Syria and Lebanon in reprisal for the Munich attack.

October 16: In Rome, Italy, Israeli operatives assassinate Wael Zwaiter, a Palestinian thought to be part of Black September. Assassinations continue until 1988 as part of the so-called Operation Wrath of God.

October 29: A plane owned by the German airline Lufthansa is hijacked, and the hijackers demand the release of the three surviving Munich attackers. Germany agrees to release them, and the three are taken to Libya. Later reports suggest that the initial hijacking was staged—that the Germans agreed to let the Munich attackers go free in order to prevent further incidents in Germany.

1973   April: In Operation Spring of Youth, special forces of the Israeli Army attack PLO camps in Lebanon, killing three top PLO leaders, among others. The attack is considered part of the revenge for the Munich massacre.

1980   Politics continue to influence the Olympics as the United States boycotts the Summer Games in Moscow, the capital of the Soviet Union, in response to the Soviet Union's invasion of Afghanistan. In reprisal, the Soviet Union boycotts the 1984 Summer Games in Los Angeles, California.

1996   The first ever Palestinian team takes part in the Summer Olympic Games in Atlanta, Georgia.

2005   The Munich massacre, and a fictionalized version of Israel's retribution for it, is the subject of *Munich,* a major Hollywood film directed by Stephen Spielberg.

2010   Abu Daoud, thought to be the mastermind of the Munich attack, dies of natural causes in Syria. Only one of the actual attackers, Jamal el-Gashey, is thought to remain alive, living in hiding in either Syria or North Africa.

2012   Olympic officials reject the latest call by survivors and family members to stage an official memorial of the 1972 massacre at the Summer Games in London, England.

FOR FURTHER READING

Books

Serge Groussard, *The Blood of Israel: The Massacre of the Israeli Athletes at the Olympics, 1972,* trans. Harold J. Salemson. New York: William Morrow, 1975.

George Jonas, *Vengeance: The True Story of an Israeli Counter-Terrorist Team.* New York: Simon and Schuster, 2005.

David Clay Large, *Munich 1972: Tragedy, Terror, and Triumph at the Olympic Games.* New York: Rowman and Littlefield, 2012.

Richard W. Pound, *Inside the Olympics: A Behind-the-Scenes Look at the Politics, the Scandals, and the Glory of the Games.* Hoboken, NJ: Wiley Publishing, 2006.

Simon Reeve, *One Day in September: The Full Story of the Munich Olympics Massacre and the Israeli Revenge Operation 'Wrath of God'.* New York: Arcade Publishing, 2011.

Barry Rubin, *Revolution Until Victory: The Politics and History of the PLO.* Cambridge, MA: Harvard University Press, 1996.

Kay Schiller and Chris Young, *The 1972 Munich Olympics and the Making of Modern Germany.* Berkeley, CA: University of California Press, 2010.

Liz Sonneborn, *Murder at the 1972 Olympics in Munich.* New York: Rosen Publishing, 2003.

Paul Taylor, *Jews and the Olympics: The Clash Between Sports and Politics.* Eastbourne, UK: Sussex Academy Press, 2004.

David C. Young, *A Brief History of the Olympic Games.* Hoboken, NJ: Wiley-Blackwell, 2005.

Periodicals

Lisa Beyer, "The Myths and Reality of Munich," *Time,* December 4, 2005.

Felix Bohr, Gunther Latsch, and Klaus Wiegrefe, "1972 Olympics Massacre: Germany's Secret Contacts to Palestinian Terrorists," *Spiegel Online,* August 28, 2012.

Paul Thomas Chamberlain, "When It Pays to Talk to Terrorists," *New York Times,* September 3, 2012.

Reid Forgrave, "Munich Still Shocks, 40 Years Later," *MSN Fox Sports,* April 17, 2012.

Richard Girling, "A Thirst for Vengeance," *The Sunday Times,* January 15, 2006.

Marvin Glassman, "Spitz Still Moved by '72 Olympics," *Palm Beach Sun Sentinel,* April 2, 2009.

Jerry Kirshenbaum, "A Sanctuary Violated," *Sports Illustrated,* September, 18, 1972.

"The Meaning of Munich," *U.S. News & World Report,* June 6, 2004.

Kenny Moore, "Munich's Message," *Sports Illustrated,* August 5, 1996.

Tom Parry, "London Olympics Hit by Super Security," *CBC News,* July 23, 2012.

Anshel Pfeffer, "Munich Families Attack International Olympic Committee President at Memorial Event," *Haaretz,* August 7, 2012.

Brendan Pittaway, "Families Sue Over Olympic Terror Deaths," *The Observer* (UK), October 2, 1999.

Shirle Povich, "The Echo of Shots That Rang Through the Dawn," *Washington Post,* July 9, 1992.

Press Association, "'Very Positive Response' to London Olympic Terror Attack Drill," *Guardian* (UK), February 22, 2012.

Simon Reeve, "Olympic Massacre: Munich—The Real Story," *The Independent* (UK), January 26, 2006.

Sharon Robb, "Munich Memories Are Rekindled: Diving Coach Recalls 1972 Tragedy," *Chicago Tribune,* July 28, 1996.

Shira Rubin, "Israel Calls for Olympic Remembrance for Murdered Athletes," *Times of Israel,* April 24, 2012.

Richard Spencer, "Black September Terrorist Who Master-Minded the Olympic Massacre Dead in Syria," *Telegraph* (UK), July 4, 2010.

Alexander Wolff, "The Mastermind," *Sports Illustrated,* August 26, 2002.

Websites

Munich 11 (www.munich11.org). This website commemorates the Israeli victims of the Munich massacre. It contains general historical information on the event and the victims as well as links to commemorative events and news on further memorials.

Munich 72 (www.olympic.org/munich-1972-summer-olympics). Part of a website maintained by the Olympic Movement, this webpage offers information, links, and film clips touching on athletic performances during the 1972 games, as well as the terrorist attack in Munich.

Political, Social, and Economic Aspects of the Olympic Games (http://olympics.pthimon.co.uk). This website, maintained in Great Britain as part of the preparations for the 2012 Summer Games in London, contains discussions of the Munich massacre as well as other instances where sports has merged with politics.

INDEX